Teens Have Feelings, Too!

100 monologs
for young performers

Deborah Karczewski

MERIWETHER PUBLISHING LTD.
Colorado Springs, Colorado

Meriwether Publishing Ltd., Publisher
P.O. Box 7710
Colorado Springs, CO 80933

Editor: Theodore O. Zapel
Typesetting: Elisabeth Hendricks
Cover design: Janice Melvin

Library of Congress Cataloging-in-Publication Data

Karczewski, Deborah, 1995-
    Teens have feelings, too : 100 monologs for young performers / Deborah Karczewski.--1st ed.
        p. cm.
    Summary: A hundred short monologs for teenage performers capture the problems and joys of the teenage years.
    ISBN 1-56608-056-8 (pbk.)
    1. Monologues--Juvenile literature. 2. Acting--Juvenile literature. [1.Monologues. 2. Acting.] I. Title: One hundred monologs for young performers. II. Title.

PN2080 .K315 2000
812'.54--dc21
                                                                    00-022176

1   2   3   4   5   00   01   02   03

Contents

Monologs for Guys (Humorous)

Monologs for Girls (Serious)

Monologs for Guys (Serious)

About the Author

Dedicated to Sabrina and Joe

Introduction

Teens have feelings, too! They may express those feelings differently; they may see the world with a unique point of view; but teens have feelings that run as deeply as those of any sensitive adult.

Teens Have Feelings, Too! is a collection of 100 monologs for people ranging from about eleven to fifteen years of age. Each monolog runs from one to three minutes, offering characters that talk like, think like and feel like real-life teens.

The individual monologs are perfect as acting exercises or audition pieces. Mixed and matched, they can be combined to form a showcase filled with moments both humorous and profound.

Any way it's used, *Teens Have Feelings, Too!* celebrates a most volatile, formative and precious time in one's life, the years between childhood and grown-up, the era of the Pre and Early Teen.

Monologs
for Girls
(Humorous)

Butterfly

1   It was so embarrassing! The butterfly was drying its
2 wings, hanging on a branch. The artist must have been six
3 years old because the color inside the cartoon wings didn't
4 reach all the way to the outline. You know what I mean?
5 Then the little cartoon cocoon started to whine in an
6 annoying voice that sounded a lot like that little kid who
7 hangs around me at the bus stop. *(Mimicking)* "Why did you
8 develop into a butterfly before I did?"
9   Well, all of the girls started cracking up. I know that
10 the point of the movie was to teach us that everyone grows
11 at different rates. I mean — duh! But instead of making the
12 girls feel better about themselves, it, like, opened up a
13 whole can of worms. Samantha — she likes to be called
14 Sam — well, she called out, "Hey, Mary, we oughta start
15 calling you Miss Butterfly!" Mary turned every color in the
16 rainbow and ran out of the room crying.
17   Her best friend, Judy, stood up and yelled, "Sam,
18 you're just jealous! You always act like a boy because you
19 know that you'll always look like one!"
20   Sam leaped over the table and was able to yank out a
21 whole fistful of Judy's hair before Mrs. Feldner, the health
22 teacher, pulled them apart. Everyone in the whole room
23 was taking sides. It sounded like feeding time at the zoo!
24   All I can say is every time I see a butterfly, I totally feel
25 the urge to laugh out loud! I think Mrs. Feldner had better
26 find a new movie! Don't you?
27
28
29
30

The Joys of Nature

1   I hate nature! My mom knows how much I despise it,
2 but she still makes me work in the garden! It's so unfair!
3 Does she enjoy torturing me like this? Her own child? Her
4 little angel? Well, that's what she calls me anyway, so how
5 can she treat me like this?
6   First she makes me wear her ratty old hat and gloves.
7 I swear if any of my friends ever saw me, they would tease
8 me for life! Then she makes me dig up those nasty, prickly
9 weeds. Give me a break! I don't know what's worse — the
10 dirt that grinds into my jeans, the bees that stare at me, or
11 the spiders that tickle my neck and make me scream!
12   That stuff is *nothing* compared to the grossest part of
13 gardening: the worms! There I am, digging away,
14 forgetting for a minute about how miserable I am, singing
15 along to my Walkman ... when all of a sudden, out
16 stretches a giant, fleshy, beige, squiggly, disgusting worm!
17 Worms have to be the creepiest creatures on earth! They
18 don't even have eyeballs! Anything that looks like that
19 deserves to live in dirt. Oh, hey, speaking of living
20 underground — why do worms feel like they have to come
21 up when it rains? Why can't they just stay out of sight? Do
22 they *like* drying up on the sidewalk? Do they get a kick out
23 of squishing under my boots?
24   Urgh! I hate worms! I can't stand gardening! Nature
25 stinks! And Mom? Sometimes she's just a ... a ... bug-
26 hugging, worm-loving, flower-planting freak!
27
28
29
30

6

College Bound

1   Hear that? No? Don't hear anything? Neither do I! Isn't
2   it fabulous? No stereo rocking the house when I'm trying
3   to do my homework ... no TV set blasting at twelve at night
4   ... no telephone ringing every ten minutes ... no tantrums
5   about how curfews are *(Mimicking)* "not fair!" ... It's
6   actually quiet! My big sister Sarah drove off to college
7   yesterday!
8   I feel like a mouse when the cat's away! Or wait — like
9   Jimmy Johnson when we had a substitute teacher last
10   week. He actually got up on his desk and started to dance!
11   I thought that the sub was gonna cough up a hairball. It
12   was too funny! No — hold on — I feel like that shrub Mom
13   found growing in the blackberry patch. It was practically
14   hidden by all those thorns and berries. But when Mom
15   transplanted it to the front yard, it actually broke out into
16   yellow flowers. This is so cool! I just want to scream out
17   loud! Who's stopping me? Not some bossy big sister! OK...
18   OK ... I will! *(Yelling)* **I'm free!!!** *(Gives a battle cry such as)*
19   **Whhooooeeeee!**
20   *(Pause)* **Wow** ... this is really great ... yup ... pretty cool
21   ... Yeah, this is ... this is ... sorta ... strange ... It's almost
22   *too* quiet. I guess it'll take some getting used to. I mean ...
23   when you live with a person every day of your life ... you
24   just sorta get used to having her around ... that's all ...
25   Maybe if I ... if I go turn on some music ... it'll ... it'll feel
26   more normal.
27   *(The actress starts to walk out. She stops suddenly. A new*
28   *idea brightens her face.)* **Hey! I wonder if Mom'll let me have**
29   **Sarah's stereo? Whhooooeeeee!**
30

Braces

1   *(The actress makes an exaggerated effort to cover her teeth*
2   *with her lips while still being careful to enunciate clearly.)*
3   No! You can't make me! Of course I know this picture
4   is for the yearbook. Whaddya think ... that I'm some kind
5   of idiot? Whaddya think ... that I'm sitting under your
6   dumb spotlights to get a tan? Of course I know what I'm
7   here for! Listen Mister, your job is to take pictures of kids,
8   not to destroy their lives!
9   I don't care what you say — there's no rule that says
10 I've got to stick out all of my teeth for the camera! All I
11 have to do is smile, right? *(Makes a strained, closed-lip smile.)*
12 There! Satisfied? Don't give me that look — I smiled. Hey,
13 a smile is a smile. OK, so I'm going to smile again, and you
14 can snap the shot so we can be out of each other's lives
15 forever. *(Makes another tight smile.)* Well, why didn't you
16 take the picture? Listen Mister, it's not like I have all day!
17   You know, it's bad enough that I have to wear these
18 stupid braces. But, do you really think that I need to be
19 reminded of them every time I look at my middle school
20 yearbook? I mean, picture this: there I am, a beautiful
21 older woman, like twenty-one or something ... and my date
22 says, "Oh honey, is this your yearbook? Which pretty little
23 girl are you? You've got to be kidding! You looked like
24 *that?!* Let me out of here!" Don't you see, Mister? If you
25 force me to make a big, giant smile now, you'll be ruining
26 the *rest of my life!*
27
28
29
30

Eye Contact

1   Oh — my — gosh! He's looking at me! He can't be
2 looking at me. It's impossible. I'm nobody, and he's really
3 really, really *somebody!* There is no way he's looking at
4 me. Nope. Uh-uh.
5   *(Opens up a textbook.)* **OK, just look casual. Yup, I'm just**
6 **reading. Just doing my homework like everyone else here**
7 **in study hall. Same ol' routine. Now slowly look in his**
8 **direction ... He is looking at me!** *(In a moment of surprised*
9 *confusion, she raises her book up in front of her face.)* **Oh man,**
10 **why did I do that? Now I look like a dork!** *(She slowly lowers*
11 *the book.)* **OK, calm down. Just thumb through the book.**
12 **Now look super interested in this page. Good — very**
13 **convincing ... Now, just take a little teeny, tiny peek to see**
14 **what he's doing.** *(She glances, sees him, and waves nervously.)*
15 **Holy smoke, I think I'm going to faint! What do I do now?**
16 **Do I wait till he says something? Maybe I should do**
17 **something to let him know that ... well ... that it's OK with**
18 **me if he has something to tell me. I mean, what if he's**
19 **waiting for some kind of a sign that I'm ... sort of ...**
20 **interested?**
21   **I know! I could ask him if he wrote down the math**
22 **assignment. Yeah! No wait ... there's no talking in study**
23 **hall. Wouldn't you know it! This is the most major**
24 **opportunity of my life, and I'm forced into silence. OK, I've**
25 **got it! I'll write him a note!** *(Reaches for her book bag.)*
26 **There's got to be some paper in here! The bell! Wait!**
27 **Where did he go?** *(Looks left and right. Disappointed, she*
28 *slumps into her chair.)* **Man, another moment ruined by the**
29 **bell!**
30

Report Card

1   *(Filing nails)* **Like, what's the big deal? I mean — hello —**
2   **it's just a report card. It's not like it's going to affect the**
3   **rest of my life or anything! Geez, Mrs. Cromwell, you sound**
4   **just like my parents! I thought you were supposed to be my**
5   **guidance counselor. Well, OK, go ahead. Guide me.**

6   **Hey, don't have a cow! It's not like any of the stuff I'm**
7   **supposed to be learning will, like, make any difference in**
8   **my life! I'm planning on going to Beauty School anyway, so**
9   **it's not like I don't have a future, you know.**

10   **I mean like, for example, how does math have anything**
11   **to do with being a beautician? Huh?** *(Listens.)* **Oh ... well, I**
12   **guess I do need to order supplies and pay salaries ... Yeah,**
13   **well, um ... science! Yeah, science! There is absolutely no**
14   **way that science — what?** *(Listens.)* **Well, OK, that's true.**
15   **Mixing hair dye does use a little teeny bit of chemistry. But**
16   **that's it — that's all that applies to — Excuse me?** *(Listens.)*
17   **I guess social studies does have some relation to taxes, but**
18   **— huh?** *(Listens.)*

19   **OK! OK! OK! I can't take it anymore! Fine! Be that**
20   **way! I'll study harder! Talk about somebody who's always**
21   **gotta get in the last word!** *(Walks to the door.)*

22   **Hey, what about English? Oh, never mind ... you win.**
23
24
25
26
27
28
29
30

Foreign Languages

1   *(Holding a test)* **I failed my first test today. I hate that**
2   **Mrs. Cheskey. She knows I can't conjugate verbs! She**
3   *knows* **I do better with multiple choice! But she purposely**
4   **made that test impossible. And you know why? Because**
5   **she hates me; that's why.**
6   **My mother's going to make me stay home this weekend**
7   **and study French. I just know it! I bet that Mrs. Cheskey**
8   **had it all planned to hand back her test the Friday before**
9   **the class dance! Yeah, that's it. It was the ultimate revenge.**
10   **French! Urgh! What's the point, anyway? It's not like**
11   **I'd ever bother going to France. There are so many better**
12   **ways to spend my money. Why would I want to go**
13   **somewhere where they're too dumb to know how to speak**
14   **a single word of English?** *(To the test)* **Yo, Mrs. Cheskey, get**
15   **a clue! You're teaching a dead language! ... Well, almost**
16   **dead, anyway. Everybody knows that Spanish is taking**
17   **over the world!**
18   **That's it! Next year I'm switching to Spanish. That'll**
19   **show her! I'll start learning a whole new subject. Yeah! All**
20   **new verbs! All new conjugation! All new ... wait a minute**
21   **... What am I — nuts? I don't want to have to begin a whole**
22   **new language! Spanish? What's with those foreigners**
23   **trying to brainwash us poor little kids?**
24   **It's un-American!**
25
26
27
28
29
30

Family Addition

1   How can Mom be pregnant? This just can't be
2 happening! First of all, she's way too old to be having
3 another kid. And besides, there's already those two
4 animals she calls my brothers! And — and that means that
5 she and Dad — no, I'm not going to think about it!
6   Where does she expect to put it — on the roof? If it's a
7 boy, I'll be outnumbered even more! But if it's a girl, I'll be
8 stuck with it in my room! A whiny, stinking, puking runt in
9 *my* space! Not only will I not get any sleep, but
10 everybody'll be in here all the time! That means I've got to
11 constantly keep my room clean! This is torture!
12   I can just imagine Mom barging in every hour to see if
13 the little tadpole is OK. Don't you think she should trust
14 me to know if the kid's all right? I mean, after helping raise
15 two brothers, I'm practically an expert! And Mrs. Meyer
16 down the street says I'm always the first girl she calls when
17 she needs a baby-sitter. She's always going on about how
18 patient I am ... how little Cindy's always asking when I'll
19 come back ...
20   Now that Cindy's a cute little kid. She's nothing like
21 those two Neanderthals Mom calls my brothers. There's
22 something special about a little girl ... You can dress her
23 up ... brush her hair ... play dolls ...
24   OK. Mom can have a baby on one condition: it's *got* to
25 be a girl!
26
27
28
29
30

Too Young for ...

1   I hate that word! It gets me so mad — so angry — so
2 ... so furious! You know what's the most annoying word in
3 my parents' vocabulary? "Tooyoungfor." You heard me.
4 It's a brand new word ... one word, three syllables.
5 Tooyoungfor. *(Spells it.)* T-O-O-Y-O-U-N-G-F-O-R. I've been
6 hearing it my whole life!
7   "You're tooyoungfor pierced ears."
8   "You're tooyoungfor shaving your legs."
9   "You're tooyoungfor makeup."
10   *(Scream of frustration such as)* **Urgh!** Today the slogan of
11 the day is, "You're tooyoungfor dating."
12   I *told* them that it's not a real date. Man! I explained
13 that it's just a bunch of us going out for fast food and a
14 movie. What's wrong with that? OK, so maybe there's only
15 four of us ... and maybe two of 'em are guys ... but can't
16 guys be just friends? Well, OK, maybe an eleven o'clock
17 movie *is* a little late ... but it's not like I go out all the time!
18 Give me a break! It's a one-shot deal!
19   I *should've* said, "Yeah? Well, Mom and Dad, I think
20 *you're* tooyoungfor turning into such party-poopers!
21 *You're* tooyoungfor becoming such old fogies! *You're*
22 tooyoungfor turning into Grandma and Grandpa!"
23   ... Why is it, I always think of the best things to say
24 *after* I've already lost the battle?
25
26
27
28
29
30

Ditz

1   Like, hi! Wassup? Do you mind if I sit here? I'm new
2 here! My name is Alexandria Hamilton, but everyone calls
3 me Honey! It's kind of funny — oops, I rhymed. *(Giggle)* Get
4 it? ... Honey? ... funny? Well, anyway, what's funny is that
5 whenever I'm around, like, a couple, and one of 'em says,
6 "Oh honey," I say, "Yes?" *(Laughs.)* It cracks me up every
7 time!
8   I really like your outfit! It looks like it cost a whole lot
9 of money! *(Giggle)* There I go again! Honey ... money! See?
10 I rhyme every time! *(Hysterical laugh)* Rhyme ... time! Oh,
11 please *(Laughing)* I'm beginning to cry!
12   I am just having the best time at this new school! Well,
13 I know it's not really new. I mean, *I'm* new, not the school.
14 Well, I'm not *new*. That'd mean I was just born or
15 something! *(Giggle)* I mean I'm new to the school. Ya know?
16 The people here are so nice! Not like at my old school. It's
17 not actually an *old* school — it was just built a few years
18 ago. But it's *my* old school. See? Because I used to go
19 there ... before I came here ... which is why that was my
20 old school and this is my new school. Get it? *(Giggle)*
21   You know what I like best about the people here? The
22 conversations. They're so stimulating! At my old school
23 people never talked about anything important, anything
24 meaningful. My old friends ... well, they weren't really old.
25 They were our age, actually, but ... Hey! Where are you
26 going! Hey! ... Was it something I said?
27
28
29
30

The Exam

1   The human brain is certainly an amazing organ! I can
2   sit here at my desk, have an entire conversation with
3   myself without anybody else knowing ... but I can't
4   remember a single thing I studied last night! Urgh!!
5   *(Smiles at someone.)* **Look calm ... Look cool ... Don't let**
6   **anyone know you've lost it, girl. Gotta keep up the image.**
7   **What's the point of end-of-the-year tests anyway? If the**
8   **teachers had done their jobs correctly, there wouldn't be**
9   **any reason to find out how much we kids know because**
10   **we'd all know everything! So when you think about it,**
11   **they're punishing us because they didn't work hard**
12   **enough! How fair is that?**
13   *(Smiles at someone else.)* **Gotta act like "Oh yeah, this**
14   **test is a piece of cake! I'm having such a good time. Aren't**
15   **you?"** *(Smiles.)*
16   **Holy Swear Word! Think, girl, think. I studied all night!**
17   **I gave up my favorite TV shows! Heck, I even turned off the**
18   **ringer on my phone! What is wrong with me?**
19   *(Smiles at someone.)* **Maybe it's just a bad case of nerves.**
20   **Breathe in. Breathe out. Breathe in. Breathe out.** *(Talking*
21   *to herself as if to a baby)* **Everything's going to be O ... K. No**
22   **matter what happens, life will go on. It's just one tiny**
23   **obstacle compared to your whole** *gihugic (Pronounced g as*
24   *in giant and huge)* **life! Ready? OK, I can do this. Go!** *(Begins*
25   *writing quickly and happily.)*
26
27
28
29
30

Party

1   *(The actress is getting ready for a party. She can either*
2   *provide props and music or mime her actions.)*
3   I hate my clothes! This one is too cutesy. I really have to
4   look mature tonight. How 'bout this one? Nah, Dad would
5   never let me out of the house in that one. Why doesn't he
6   get with the times? OK ... found it! Not too frilly ... not too
7   skimpy ... makes me look a whole lot older ... Bingo!
8   *(Dancing to music)* I am going to dance till my feet fall
9   off. If the guys don't ask me, I'll ask them. I plan on
10   dancing till my dad rings that doorbell, and even then I
11   might not stop. These feet are gonna ... wait! Shoes! Oh
12   man, I hate my shoes! Should I go for comfort or for
13   image? Heels? Wedges? Sandals? Straps? How 'bout this
14   pair? Nah. Those'd weigh me down, and tonight I'm gonna
15   fly! I'm gonna sail! I'm gonna twirl! Hold it ... Ah! Shoe
16   perfection! These'll look so major cool with this outfit!
17   I can't wait to see Valerie's face when she checks me
18   out tonight. She always has to be the focus of every party.
19   When she gets an eyeful of this outfit, her hair'll stand on
20   end! Hair! I hate my hair! Ponytail? Too sporty. Slicked
21   back? No — too lifeguard. Do I wear it up? No — too
22   librarian. Pigtails? Heck no, I'd look like Pippi
23   Longstocking. The casual wind-blown look? Hey, not bad.
24   Not bad at all! Looks fun-loving, free-spirited, ready-to-go
25   ... Oh yeah, this is the look all right.
26   Valerie Hoffman, eat your heart out! I've got the
27   moves; I've got the dress; I've got the shoes; I've got the
28   hair ... I am it, girl! Valerie's gonna cry so hard that her
29   mascara will run down her face like ... like ... Mascara?
30   Makeup! Oh no, I hate my makeup!

Healthy Eating

1   Got a candy bar? Please? Look, I'm begging you. Potato
2 chips? I'd kill for a cookie. Help me! I need junk food!
3   I used to be such a happy kid. Oh, those were the days.
4 I remember when I'd open up my brown paper bag at lunch
5 time, and I'd find a peanut butter and marshmallow fluff
6 sandwich, nice and gooey ... chocolate, whole milk, extra
7 creamy ... and a yummy cupcake with sprinkles on top.
8 Mmmmm, I can almost taste it just thinking about it!
9   But now that Mom's on this health-kick of hers, I'm
10 wasting away! There's nothing to thicken my blood against
11 the cold, cruel winter! I'm starving to death! Please ... just
12 one little pudding cup? I'll be your best friend!
13   OK, how about a trade? Let's see what we have here.
14 Hey, this is your lucky day! What about this puny, pale,
15 purple plum? It's pesticide free! Oh — what'll you give me
16 for this tempting sandwich? What kind? ... Um ... lettuce ...
17 tomato ... and tofu. But hey, it's got a nice helping of non-
18 fat mayo, so it's not too dry! I know — check out what's in
19 my thermos ... Well, I'm not sure what kind it is. Lemme
20 take a sip. *(Coughs and gags.)* Must've gone down the wrong
21 pipe. Oh, you've got to try this stuff. My mom is so
22 creative with that new juicer she got for the holidays. What
23 kind of juice? ... Uh, well ... it tastes like a combination of
24 carrot, celery, pineapple, and a touch of ... garlic. Really
25 thins the blood. Great for the heart.
26   Oh please, please, please! Throw a dog a bone!
27 Brownie? Processed meat? I'd even settle for a fried pork
28 rind! Gosh, I think I'm about to be the first person who
29 ever died of healthy eating!
30

Snob

1   I ... am ... like ... speechless! How can anyone — anyone
2 who matters, anyway — accuse *me* of being a *snob*?
3   I mean, get real. I am the friendliest person in the
4 entire class. Remember? I'm the one who handed out
5 Godiva chocolates to the whole homeroom! I even gave
6 one to that girl who wears the ripped jeans, and I don't
7 even, like, know her name!
8   I know ... you're just jealous! Look, I *would've* invited
9 you to my pool party. Really, I would've, but I was trying
10 to protect you. And *this* is how you show your gratitude?
11 I know you don't have that much money — not that it
12 matters, heaven knows — and I didn't want you to have to
13 worry about buying a new bathing suit, that's all. Here I
14 am worrying about *your* feelings and *your* reputation ...
15 and how do you thank me? By calling me a *snob*!
16   ... Well, just to show you who's the bigger person — I'm
17 not talking about actual size, of course, 'cause you sure
18 have me beat there — but just to show you who's the most
19 un-snobby ... I forgive you. My mama always tells me to
20 forgive and forget ... especially if the person is a poor, little
21 chubby girl. It is up to us, those blessed in society, to set an
22 example for those beneath us. *(Flips hair and saunters off.)*
23
24
25
26
27
28
29
30

Snoring

1   *(Big yawn)* **I have never been so tired in my life! That's**
2   **fact number one. And I am never, ever, never-ever-ever**
3   **going to the shore with my cousins again. That is definitely**
4   **fact number two!** *(Yawn)*
5   **Being an only child, I was so thrilled when Aunt Daisy**
6   **asked Mom and Dad if I'd like to join her family for a week**
7   **at their beach cabin. I thought, "Yay! Seven days of**
8   **swimming and biking and fishing and boating!" Well, I was**
9   **right ... about the days that is. The problem, though, was**
10   **the nights.**
11   **Picture this: an eency-weency room with two sets of**
12   **bunk beds. Cozy, you say? Wait, I haven't finished. Picture**
13   **my twin boy-cousins in one pair of beds, and my cousin**
14   **Barbara in the other. Nice arrangement? Wait — that's just**
15   **the beginning. Here's the killer part: all three — snore.**
16   *Snore* **isn't a strong enough word. Imagine three saws**
17   **all grinding through logs at the same time. No! Think of**
18   **three locomotives screeching to a sudden stop. Wait, that's**
19   **not awful enough — pretend you heard an army of**
20   **warthogs having a huge battle over a colony of bugs. Or ...**
21   **or a tornado ripping through a village! Or the sound a**
22   **skyscraper makes when it's being demolished, and the**
23   **building falls in on itself, crashing to the ground! ... Picture**
24   **seven long, endless nights, staring at the ceiling, listening**
25   **to sounds that would make a foreign spy confess and beg**
26   **for mercy.** *(Yawn)*
27   **Fact number three: I'm goin' to sleep, now ... all alone**
28   **... in my lonely, little room ... in my tiny, twin bed ... maybe**
29   **for a year ...** *(Yawn)*
30

Baby Sitter Bimbo

1   Oh, don't be sad, little Ellie. Your mommy and daddy
2 will be back real soon. And while they're gone, we can get
3 to know each other! Oh come on, cutie pie, stop staring at
4 the time. Like they say, "A watched clock never toils" ... or
5 something like that.
6   All they're doing is having dinner and seeing a movie.
7 Know what? Your mommy left us some sandwiches in the
8 kitchen. Let's go eat! No? Aren't you hungry? Aw, you can
9 have a *little* bit, can't you? You know, "Good things
10 happen to those who ate!" OK, sweetie, I guess there's no
11 point in forcing you. "You can lead a horse to water, but it
12 might make him stink."
13   Watcha laughing at, Ellie? Haven't you ever heard of
14 proverbs? Wise sayings? Lucky for me, my mom raised me
15 by 'em. There's a deep moral to be learned in almost every
16 situation. Even when things seem at their worst, "There's
17 always hope at the end of your elbow." And do you know
18 why, honey? Because "Every cloud has a silver hiney." Oh
19 yes, it's true.
20   So don't be sad, little Ellie. Your mommy and daddy
21 will be back soon. Don't be upset that they're at some
22 fancy restaurant without you. We can have as much fun as
23 they're having! "The grass is always greener, but it's not as
24 wide." Oh, I know! Let's play some games! "He who laughs
25 last has a real blast!"
26
27
28
29
30

Pisces

1   I'm starting to think there's something to this astrology
2 thing. Don't tell Mom, though. She's the queen of
3 "Everything Has a Scientific Explanation." If she knew I
4 believed in horoscopes, she'd pop a cork!
5   So anyway, my friends and I started looking at the
6 horoscope section of the newspaper basically as a goof.
7 Y'see, library period in school is such a giant drag. We had
8 to find *something* to keep us from going insane. I mean,
9 how much can one person talk about the Dewey Decimal
10 System? So we'd look up our signs, find out if this was our
11 lucky day, joke about who we'd marry ... you know — the
12 typical stuff.
13   Well, to get to the point ... today I asked Brian if he
14 liked me. He said yeah, but only like a friend. Can I tell you
15 how embarrassing that was? My friends had been pushing
16 me all week long. "Go ahead and ask him," they'd say. "He
17 really likes you. It's soooo obvious." So after about a
18 billion phone calls, they finally convinced me. I got up all
19 of my nerve, just to look like the world's biggest loser!
20   Well, to make a long story short, I ran home, totally in
21 tears, and flung myself on my bed. I must have gone
22 through a whole box of tissues. Finally, I had the idea that
23 maybe a nice, hot shower would make me feel better. So I
24 took an extra long one, complete with exfoliating scrub
25 and after-bath splash. And you know what? I feel so much
26 better!
27   That's when it hit me! I'm a Pisces! Well, don't you get
28 it? It's the sign of the fish! Fish love water! *I* love water!
29 How cool is that? There is definitely more to this astrology
30 stuff than meets the eye!

Driving with Pappy Joe

1   Is the room spinning, or is it me? You have to excuse
2 me if I seem spacey. I've just been out driving with Pappy
3 Joe!
4   It started innocently enough. He was so proud when I
5 showed him my report card that he said he wanted to take
6 his favorite granddaughter out for an extra-large ice cream
7 sundae. Well, it's not like I'd ever turn down an offer for
8 ice cream! ... Big mistake ... big, *big* mistake.
9   I should have realized that something was off when we
10 buckled in. Pappy pulled his seat so far up that his chin
11 was almost touching the wheel. But before I had a chance
12 to think about it, the car screeched out of the driveway. I
13 don't know what came over my grandfather, but instantly
14 he turned into the Pappy of Doom ... Pappy from the Land
15 of the Near-sighted ... Pappy, Road Warrior!
16 *(Using a crazed, old man's voice)* "What're all these
17 people doing out on the road? Get outta my ding-dong
18 way! Dagnabbit! Where'd you get your license — off a
19 cereal box? Raffen-smaffen-ritzen-fratzen! When's the
20 town plannin' on paving these roads? I keep hitting the
21 bleep-bleep potholes!"
22   "Uh ... Pappy Joe," I gasped nervously, "I think we're
23 riding up the curb!"
24   "Oh sorry," he answered. "They ought to widen the
25 blankety-blank street!"
26   I don't know how we got to the ice cream parlor alive,
27 what flavor I ate, or how we managed to get back in one
28 piece. All I know is next time Pappy Joe starts feeling his
29 sweet tooth ... I'm baking cookies!
30

Ferris Wheel

1   It's bad enough that those friends of mine dared me to
2 go on this Monster Ferris Wheel when they know how
3 much I hate heights ... but to top it off, the ticket guy cut
4 the ride line right behind me! That means *I'm* up here ...
5 and those sorry excuse for friends are way ... way ... way
6 down there! Aaaahhh! *(Or similar blood-curdling scream)*

7   *I'm — not — happy!* This car I'm riding in goes up and
8 up and up and up ... and just when I feel comfortable ... I
9 fall down and down and down! It's never-ending! I really
10 regret having a funnel cake appetizer, cotton candy dinner,
11 and snow cone dessert! *Yow!* Every time the ferris wheel
12 goes down, my stomach stays up!

13   It serves me right! If I hadn't screamed so much on the
14 Tilt o'Whirl, they'd never have gotten the idea to dare me
15 to go on *this* rusty machine of doom! Me and my big
16 mouth! I didn't want to look like a *total* baby, y'know. I
17 had already said "no way" to the roller coaster and "You're
18 outta your mind" to the Loop the Loop! It was between the
19 Monster Wheel or the Tower of Terror. They dared me to
20 pick one or be named the group scaredy cat. I had no
21 choice!

22   What's wrong with going to a carnival and playing safe
23 little games like Ring Toss or Duck Pond? Who says real
24 women ride death machines? I admit it! I'm a coward! Sue
25 me!

26   Oooohhh boy! Here we go again! Up and up and up!
27 Moment at the top to breathe. And then ... Aaaahhhhh!
28
29
30

Gross Habits

1   So, I tried out this really wild game to make my family
2 reunion, like, go faster, you know? It's kinda like solitaire
3 'cause you play it by yourself, but you don't use cards.
4 Warning — it's super fun, but also mega disgusting. I just
5 thought I'd better prepare you, in case you get sick easily
6 or anything like that. It's called ... Gross Habits.
7   What you do is ... well ... you know all those times you
8 have to sit politely like a nice young lady and listen to a
9 whole bunch of boring stories that just go in one ear and
10 out the other? Like who had what operation ... or what life
11 was like in the good ol' days ... or every ingredient on the
12 face of the earth that you can put into a casserole? Well,
13 what you do is put on a real interested face. You know —
14 make your lips into a half smile and nod every now and
15 then. Next, tune out all the talking, and just focus in on
16 people's gross habits!
17   You won't believe what you discover! For example, my
18 Aunt Zelda keeps her hanky in her cleavage! I'm serious!
19 She'll be talking away, reach into you-know-where, blow
20 her nose, and then put it back! And Grandpa Nate? He
21 must live with a constant wedgie, because every few
22 minutes, when he thinks nobody's looking, he ... well ...
23 *de*-wedgies himself! My Dad's cousin Al cleans his ear ...
24 and then wipes his finger under the cushions of the couch!
25 His daughter Zoie pulls out one of her long hairs when
26 something gets stuck between her teeth ... and uses it as
27 dental floss! I'm telling you, it's too, too funny!
28   Take my advice, the best way to go to a family reunion
29 and live to talk about it instead of collapsing of total
30 boredom is playing Gross Habits. It really works!

Fan Mail

1   *(The actress, reading a movie magazine, gives a loud,*
2 *swooning sigh.)* **He ... is ... so ... gorgeous! Have you ever**
3 **looked into eyes so blue? Have you ever seen such blonde**
4 **hair? Teeth that white? A build that perfect?** *(Swooning sigh)*
5 **Look! The magazine lists the address of his fan club.**
6 **Should I?** *(Giggle)* **You go, girl!**
7   *(Rummages for pen and paper.)* **OK. All set. Now ... how**
8 **do I begin?** *(Reading as she writes)* **Dear ... Oh, now what**
9 **should I call him? I need to find a really romantic**
10 **nickname. OK — got it!**
11   **Dear ... Work of Art,**
12   **I just had to write to you to tell you how much I like**
13 **...** *(She crosses out a word)* **how much I** *adore* **your movies. I**
14 **keep a picture of you under my pillow at night. It's a little**
15 **chewed up because my cat Flufster likes you, too.**
16   **If you** *ever* **need anything, I would be at your**
17 **command. I could do your laundry ... quiz you on your**
18 **lines ... fetch your coffee ... all for the honor of being**
19 **allowed to look at you!**
20   **If you are ever in my town, here's how to reach me.**
21 *(Scribbles address silently.)*
22   **Sincerely** *(Crosses it out)* **...** *Adoringly,* **Your Servant.**
23   **There! I hear being on a movie set is a really lonely life.**
24 **I betcha the poor guy never even gets any mail. Better send**
25 **this off right away!** *(Scampers off.)*
26
27
28
29
30

Parade

1   **Yahooo!** *(Or similar whoop of glee)* **What a major rush!**
2   *(Waving periodically to the crowd)* **This is the first time I've**
3   **seen a parade from the inside out!** *(Yells.)* **Oh ... Oh, hi,**
4   **Mom! She looks so proud.** *(Laughs.)* **My little brother's**
5   **arm's gonna fall off from waving so hard. Here, punko,**
6   **have some candy!** *(Pantomimes throwing candy from a bag*
7   *into the crowd.)* **Lookit 'em all diving for candy like it was**
8   **gold! Kids are such a riot. They crack me up.**
9   **Yup, the Swim Team is the greatest!** *(Covers face.)* **Aw,**
10   **Dad, not the video camera — how juvenile! Oh, OK, smile**
11   **for the camera.** *(Smiles.)* **See? I'm smiling! Yup, the**
12   **Smithtown Marlins won the county meet! And now, here**
13   **we are in the Fourth of July parade.** *(Yelling)* **Oh, hi, Amy!**
14   **Meet me at the end of the parade! ... I've never been on a**
15   **fire engine before. It's the coolest! Kinda loud. Hard to**
16   **hear yourself think!**
17   **Wow, you can see everything from up here. There's the**
18   **high school band. Those new red uniforms look totally**
19   **classy. I can't wait to join up in a couple years! And there's**
20   **the Boy Scouts. Poor Jimmy looks boiling hot carrying their**
21   **banner. Hmmm, he's even cute when he's soggy! Oh, and**
22   **there's the Mayor!** *(Yells.)* **Hi, Mr. Franklin! He's my neighbor.**
23   **You know, I used to really bad-mouth this little town. I**
24   **used to complain that there was nothing to do ... nowhere to**
25   **go. Everybody knows everybody else's business. But today?**
26   **Today everything looks totally different! Maybe it's winning**
27   **the meet. Maybe it's bein' on a huge fire engine. Whatever it**
28   **is ...** *(Yelling)* **I love you, Smithtown! Here kids, have some**
29   **candy!** *(Throws and laughs.)* **Kids, you gotta love 'em.**
30

House Key

1   It was nice of your mom to ask me to supper. *(Snorts in*
2 *and wipes nose on sleeve.)* I feel really stupid forgetting my
3 house key and all. *(Obnoxious laugh)*
4   Jeepers, we've been neighbors for years, but this is the
5 first time I've ever been in your house. It sure is nice sitting
6 on a couch that doesn't have a plastic slip cover on it. In
7 my house it gets so humid that when I stand up, the plastic
8 stays stuck to my thighs! *(Obnoxious laugh)* Ooops, I hope
9 it's not too forward to say "thigh" to a boy. But hey,
10 everybody's got 'em: people, animals ... in fact, it's the
11 tastiest part of the chicken! *(Laughs, snorts, wipes nose.)*
12   I don't want to sound aggressive or anything ... but I'm
13 kinda glad I forgot my key. I finally have the chance to ...
14 get to know you. You're cute. You're even cuter than your
15 Scotty dog, but I won't try to scratch your belly! *(Laughs.)*
16   Aw, I know you have your eye on Beth Watkins, but
17 that's because you've never had the chance to know what
18 I'm really like. I'm amazingly fun to have around. And now
19 that you know I'm alive and all ... we can do all sorts of
20 things together.
21   If you're interested, I would enjoy showing you my
22 collection of beetles from around the world. It's not your
23 typical bug collection — oh no. I have specimens that
24 range from your ordinary garden variety to one that I had
25 flown in from the Amazon that's as big as my hand! I even
26 have a few samples of edible beetles! They're especially
27 delicious covered in chocolate. In fact, I usually carry a few
28 around with me in my pocket ... oh look! *(Laughs, snorts.)*
29 It's my house key! It must've been in my pocket the whole
30 time ... silly me.

Earth Mother

1   I'm everyone's best friend. I'm the one everybody
2 confides in. I'm the person everyone goes to for solving
3 problems. And I hate it!
4   It's an incredible pressure being the *Earth Mother* for
5 all my friends! Might as well take a cattle brand and burn
6 the letters E M into my forehead — Earth Mother. Go to
7 Earth Mother when your parents don't appreciate you.
8 Seek Earth Mother when your teachers are unfair. Earth
9 Mother is kind! Earth Mother is sensitive! Earth Mother
10 always understands! It drives me nuts!
11   Now that everyone depends on me, I feel like I have to
12 … live up to the image, you know? I've sort of *become*
13 what everyone expects me to be, what they want me to be.
14 And I hate it because it's dishonest.
15   I *want* to say, "Stop whining and your parents won't
16 call you immature!" or "Grow up and just do your darn
17 homework!" or "Face it — he's never going to like you
18 unless you have a personality transplant!" But instead, I do
19 a lot of smiling and agreeing and nodding. Then I give out
20 hugs and tissues and lucky pennies.
21   I've got everybody conned. Everybody goes home
22 feeling better about themselves … everybody, that is,
23 except Earth Mother.
24
25
26
27
28
29
30

Zipped Up

1   OK Ma, you *promised* not to say a single word until
2 I've gotten everything out, right? But if past practice is any
3 clue, you won't be able to handle that. Uh-uh! Shhh! See
4 what I mean? I *know* you, Ma. So, the way I've got it
5 figured is that we need a signal ... a symbolic signal ...
6 whenever you need to be reminded about your promise.
7 OK? Now ... pretend your mouth is your purse and your
8 lips are the zipper. Uh-uh! Shhh! Work with me here, Ma.
9 OK, now when I pull my thumb and forefinger across my
10 mouth like this ... it means to zip up. Got it?
11   Well ... what I want to talk about is getting a dog. Uh-
12 uh! *(Does the zipper signal.)* 'Cause whenever I've brought it
13 up before, I've never had the chance to give my side of the
14 argument. You get all hairy and upset and start flapping
15 your wings like a big vulture! *(Zip signal)*
16   Ma, I know that before now I was too young for a dog.
17 I do. I understand that you thought it'd be one more
18 headache for you to handle, almost like having a whole
19 'nother kid. But Ma ... I'm responsible now. I would feed it
20 first thing every morning. You know I'm really good at
21 getting up by my alarm clock now, right? I even give Billy
22 his instant oatmeal when I get up before you do. If I can
23 feed my brother, I can certainly feed a dog! And I'll do all
24 the walking by myself: once in the morning, then the
25 second I get of the school bus, again after dinner, and
26 finally at bed time. See? I have it all figured out. Whaddya
27 think?
28   ... Oh, OK, very funny, Mom. You can unzip your purse
29 now!
30

Blemish

1   It's there. No, I'm *not* going to show it to you. Trust me
2 ... it's there, but I've got it covered by my hair. It is the
3 ugliest ... most disgusting ... giant ... monster of a zit
4 you've ever seen.
5   I'm so embarrassed. I'm *so* humiliated. It's practically
6 the size of my face! I could just lie down and die right on
7 this spot ... but I won't ... because if I do ... when they're
8 preparing my body ... they'll see it under my hair ... and
9 the last memory everyone will have of me is ... is that
10 humongous, nauseating zit.
11   What I *should* do ... what I *should* do is take a pen and
12 draw two eyes on it. Then I could tell everybody it's a
13 visiting alien that's decided to hang out on my forehead.
14 It'd be a lot less scary that way. People'd be much more
15 willing to look at a cute, little space creature than the zit
16 of the century.
17   I know, I could enter it in *Ripley's Believe It or Not*. I
18 can just see the caption now: "Young Girl Grows Pimple
19 the Size of a Hamster!"
20   Mom says I'm making a big deal out of nothing. She
21 says everybody gets "blemishes" as she calls them. She
22 says that I should just go downstairs and nobody will even
23 notice it. Yeah, right. You go tell Mom to put my dinner in
24 the refrigerator. I'm not budging. Me and my little alien are
25 staying right up here in my room ... forever!
26
27
28
29
30

Pink

1   *(Nervous)* Uh ... Mom? Have you been following the
2 latest fashion craze? No? Oh ... well, let me tell you about
3 it. The biggest thing in fashion these days is *pink!*
4   Now, I know that I've been rebelling against pink lately,
5 but I've been so wrong! I know I made you take all my old
6 pink stuff to the rummage sale. It's true I had a tantrum
7 about not wanting to be a little girl anymore. I appreciate
8 you spending spring vacation wallpapering over my pink
9 walls. But ... it was all a big mistake.
10   Pink is *in* now, Mom. Pink is *hot.* Pink is all the rage!
11 It's *now!* It's *happening!* It's wild and crazy! Pink
12 separates the divas from the dolts! It's all over the media!
13 Everybody's wearing it! From girls my age ... to boys ... to
14 mature and beautiful women like yourself ... to
15 businessmen! Oh yes, Mom, pink is the classiest color to
16 wear with a suit and tie these days.
17   ... Which is a good thing ... actually ... because pink is
18 ... pink is the color of ... our laundry. Oh now, Mom, before
19 you freak, it was an accident! I separated the whites from
20 the colors just like you taught me ... but ... I forgot about
21 the red bandanna in the pocket of my white jeans! And ...
22 and when I opened up the washing machine, everything
23 was ... pink!
24   ... Mom, how do you think Daddy will react to pink
25 boxer shorts?
26
27
28
29
30

Monologs
for Guys
(Humorous)

Peak Moment

1   I bet it doesn't get any better than this! I know I'll never
2 feel this great again. I just wish I could video tape my
3 insides, my feelings. If there was only some way to trap
4 this moment in a box and keep it for later!
5   The best part was the applause. I really could *feel* that
6 the whole room liked my music ... liked me! And the guys
7 in my class were stomping their feet while everyone was
8 clapping. The floor sort of rumbled. It was so cool! If I
9 could just bottle that shaking! That's what real happiness
10 feels like ... a jiggling in the feet. Then the vibrations travel
11 all the way up until even your brain tingles!
12   All those years I'd be picked last for teams in gym
13 class ... all those times I felt like there was something
14 wrong with me because I was better at piano than soccer
15 ... I felt that I was some kind of weirdo because I'd rather
16 be making music than putting on football pads.
17   When the music teacher asked me to play for the class,
18 I started to sweat. Oh man, now I'd *really* be the joke of
19 the school. But there was no way out of it. So I played. If
20 my life was going to end anyway, I might as well play my
21 guts out. So I did.
22   And that's when it happened. The cheers! The girls
23 were looking at me like I was some kind of TV star! The
24 boys were shouting my name! They started stomping like
25 crazy!
26   Oh what the heck, I'm just gonna enjoy this feeling
27 while it lasts!
28
29
30

Roommate

1 OK you little slug, here's the plan. If I have to be stuck
2 with a little punk brother in *my* room, then *you* have to
3 follow the rules. Got it?

4 It's bad enough that I'm gonna have to be tortured by
5 a stinky, whiny, bottle-sucking baby in the house, but to
6 give up half of my room? ... to the brat of the century? ...
7 Arghhh! *(Or some noise of frustration)* **This is worse than
8 being stung by killer wasps! It's like being eaten by
9 cannibals while I'm still alive! It's ... it's ... like having to
10 clean the litter box of a giant Bengal Tiger!**

11 So here's the rules, Turkey. One: observe the row of sock
12 balls making a line down the middle of the floor. You stay on
13 *your* side of the sock line. Understand? Well, OK ... you can
14 cross to go to the bathroom ... but only once a night.

15 Two: my stuff is *my* stuff. You touch *anything* and
16 you're asking for it. See?

17 Three: when I want my privacy, I'll put a sign on the
18 outside of the door ... something like ... "Anyone Under
19 This Height Stay Out!" If you want to come in, you can
20 knock on the door and say, "Oh Great One, may I enter?"
21 And maybe, just maybe ... if you're good, I'll let ya.

22 Hey, I know ... let's give it a try. You go outside the
23 bedroom door. Yeah, that's good. Now shut the door.
24 That's right. OK, now say, "Oh Great One, may I enter?"
25 *(Listens.)* I can't hear you. Say it louder ... Hey, pinhead, I
26 can't hear you! *(Pause, followed by a look of shock)* **What's
27 that?** *(Talking sweetly through the door)* **Dad? Oh, nothing,
28 Dad. We're just playing a game! Sure, he can come in any
29 time he wants, cute little guy!** *(Pause)* **Whew! That was a
30 close one!**

Mind Reader

1   I swear she can read minds! No, I'm not kidding!
2   there's something up with my mom! OK, you can make all
3   the screwy faces you want, but she's got some sort of ... of
4   ... power or something!
5   Yeah, well if you don't believe me, explain this one.
6   Every day when I'm getting ready for bed, she tells me to
7   brush my teeth, right? Well, when I say, "I already did,"
8   she says, "Brian, get yourself right into that bathroom and
9   brush them, young man." OK, OK, I can see it in your face.
10 you're thinking that "That's just a Mom Thing," but wait'll
11 you hear this. I've been testing her out, ya see.
12   First, I run water in the sink like I'm brushing. Then, I
13 wet my toothbrush while I make all kinds of gargley noises
14 like this. *(Makes sounds.)* Finally, I suck on a candy cane so
15 I smell all minty fresh. So what happens? Even before I
16 have a chance to tell her I've brushed, Mom stomps into
17 my room and says, "Brian, either you brush right, or you
18 can kiss your video games good-bye!"
19   Not convinced? You want to tell me how she knows
20 there's dirty clothes under my mattress without even
21 walking in the room? Huh? Huh? Can you explain how she
22 can tell when I still have homework left when she doesn't
23 have a clue what the teacher assigned? See? It's ... like ...
24 weird!
25   And I can tell Dad's suspicious, too, even though he
26 won't admit it. He'll say, "Honey —" I hate when he talks
27 all mushy like that. Well anyway, he'll say, "Honey, I can't
28 find my belt." And she knows exactly where it is! Once I
29 even tried stealing his favorite brown belt and hiding it
30 under the couch. So the next day when he yelled, "Honey,

 1   (Yuk!) have you seen my belt?" — she didn't even blink.
 2   She said, "I bet the cat pushed it under the furniture."
 3   Huh? Huh? And you thought I was making this all up!
 4   I tried, I mean, I *really* tried to warn Dad about her,
 5   but he just laughed and said, "Oh, Brian, give me a
 6   break." You know what I think? I think it's hypnotism.
 7   Yup, she's got some power-hold over him. But you just
 8   wait. One of these days I'll catch 'er when she's off
 9   guard. It's just a matter of time!
10
11
12
13
14
15
16
17
18
19
20
21
22
23
24
25
26
27
28
29
30
31
32
33
34
35

Socks

1   Heck no, Mrs. Laskey, I'm not crying. It's just my
2 allergies kicking up. That's how come I asked if I could go
3 to the boys' room. I didn't want to have to blow my nose
4 in front of the whole room. You know how it is.
5   Yeah, I'm sorry I missed that story you were reading to
6 the class. If you lend me the book, I swear I'll read it by
7 tomorrow. I guess I *was* out of the room for a long time.
8 When I start sneezing, sometimes it takes me a long time
9 to ... I'm sorry, Mrs. Laskey. No, I'm OK — really ... The
10 truth is, Mrs. Laskey, I ... I just didn't want my friends to
11 ... well, I mean, the guys to ... to ... see me upset.
12   No, no you didn't do anything! Really! It was that ...
13 that little horse in the story. You were reading about that
14 boy, and how he was petting his horse's neck ... begging it
15 not to die ... and ... and I just had to get out — fast.
16   I know that a horse is way different from a dog, but I
17 just couldn't help thinking about Socks. Yeah, the vet had
18 to put my dog to sleep last weekend. Socks was real old.
19 He could barely even walk anymore ... but he was mine ...
20 and I miss him ... a real lot.
21   Please don't tell anybody, Mrs. Laskey. It's not ... well
22 ... cool for a guy to get all gushy over a dog. I'll be fine by
23 tomorrow. Really. And Mrs. Laskey? It was nice that you
24 didn't, well, hug me or anything. *(Walks slowly toward the*
25 *door.)* OK ... well ... bye ... and thanks.
26
27
28
29
30

Birth

1   My dog had puppies this morning. I don't think I've
2   ever gone through so many different changes in one
3   morning! I feel like I ran a marathon, but heck, it was my
4   dog Windy who did all the work!
5   When my dad first told me that it was actually
6   happening, I was like, "No way, I'm getting as far away
7   from here as I can!" Then I looked at Windy, saw the state
8   she was in, and started to panic! I thought, "Oh my gosh,
9   she's going to have puppies! What if something goes
10 wrong? Why don't we get her to the vet? Why isn't Mom
11 doing anything?" That's when it all started to happen.
12   Now, don't get me wrong. I took Health Class like
13 everyone else. It's not like I didn't know how babies are
14 born. But hearing about it is totally different from seeing
15 it with your own eyes. I went from, "Gross! How disgusting
16 can you get?!" to "Yowch! I can't believe they're actually
17 *born* that way!" to "Puppies are hairless and sticky!" to
18 "Ooohhh, aren't they the cutest, little things you've ever
19 seen?"
20   You should have seen the way Windy cleaned them and
21 took care of them. I was so proud of her, I could have
22 busted a gut! Gee, if I get this emotional when puppies are
23 born, what am I gonna be like when I'm a father?
24
25
26
27
28
29
30

Maid Day

1   Could you explain something to me? *Why* do we spend
2 all morning *every other* Wednesday cleaning the house ...
3 for the *maid*? Isn't there something wrong with that logic?
4   Every cleaning day my house is like a whirlwind, a
5 tornado really. Books are shoved into any empty corner.
6 Clothes are smooshed under the furniture. Toys are flying!
7 Everyone is going nuts!
8   *(The actor mimics a variety of voices.)*
9   My mom screams, "How do you expect the maid to
10 clean if your junk is all over the place?"
11   I yell, "Isn't cleaning *her* job?!"
12   My dad bellows, "You have two working parents. All we
13 ask is that you put away your own garbage!"
14   My little brother whines, "Then how come Mom's
15 always putting away *your* stuff, Dad?"
16   Then Dad howls, "You're grounded!"
17   You know, crazy as it sounds, sometimes I think it just
18 might be easier to clean my own darn room. *(He thinks*
19 *about it, then shakes his head.)* **Nah!**
20
21
22
23
24
25
26
27
28
29
30

Knock Yourself Out

1   OK, OK, I know that I'm opening myself up for all sorts
2 of teasing ... but I really like her. OK, lay it on me.
3   Come on, it's not like I haven't already heard it from
4 my brother when he picked up the phone. *(Mimics brother.)*
5 "Oh lover-boy, sweetheart, your crush is on the phone! Oh,
6 stud-muffin! Oh, honey-pie!" Yeah, he won't think it's so
7 funny when he washes his hair with Mom's hand lotion
8 tonight. Oops, how did the labels switch like that? Beats
9 me! So if you want to say something, go ahead. I don't
10 even know where your bathroom is, so your shampoo is
11 safe as can be!
12   No, seriously ... it's the first time in my life that I've met
13 a girl I want to talk to. It's weird. One day girls are a pain
14 in the neck ... and then ... over night ... I find one who I
15 actually wanna call on the phone! I mean ... I'm watching
16 TV, and then it reminds me of something really funny that
17 happened at school and ... and I sorta have this ... this
18 urge to call her up and tell her about it. And then she
19 sounds like she's kinda glad that I called. You know? It's
20 nice. It makes me feel ... well ... important. And when I'm
21 all exhausted after baseball practice, and all stressed out
22 about homework, and ... and annoyed at my brother ... it's
23 nice to talk to somebody who thinks I'm ... you know ...
24   So, if you want to call me names, knock yourself out. I
25 really don't care ... not much, anyway.
26
27
28
29
30

Karate Kid

1   *(A * indicates when the actor should listen to the "other*
2 *guy." The actor is yelling as though his opponent is across the*
3 *street.)*
4   **Yeah? * Yeah? * Oh yeah? * Come over here and say**
5 **that to my face! * Huh? * Hey, if you're such a big man,**
6 **bring your butt over here! * Heck no, *you* come over here!**
7 *** I'm not going over there. You come over here!**
8   **You big coward! * Yeah, I'm talkin' to you! Big mama's**
9 **boy! You a little baby or something? Wimp! You a girl? A**
10 **pretty little girl? Right, Princess?**
11   *(Out loud to himself)* **Omigosh, he's coming over! What**
12 **do I do?**
13   *(Yelling again)* **I'd better warn you, Dude, that I take**
14 **karate! * 'Course I'm serious! Been taking lessons for three**
15 **years! Sure have! Three days a week after school! Got a**
16 **couple of belts, too!** *(Does some karate moves while making*
17 *loud noises.)* **See? So if … if you wanna back off, I'd**
18 **understand. *I* sure wouldn't want to mess with me if *I* was**
19 **you. Yeah, I'd just slowly back away and … and forget the**
20 **whole thing. Yup … I'd just … I'd just …**
21   **Hey … did ya hear that? I think it was your mother**
22 **calling! * No, I'm not crazy! Hear it? That's your mother! ***
23 **No, it's not *my* mother; it's *your* mother. * Is *not!* * Well,**
24 **maybe the best thing is if we both check home and then**
25 **meet up after supper! * No, *you* get here at seven o'clock**
26 **sharp! Don't you worry 'bout *me! I'll* be here!** *(Walking Off-*
27 *stage)* *** Oh yeah? * Yeah? * Yeah?** *(Gone)*
28
29
30

Speed Demon

1   I'm gonna be a race car driver ... or maybe a
2 motorcycle driver ... or race a speed boat! Whatever it is,
3 I can guarantee you that I'm gonna be *fast!*
4   The times I feel the most alive, the most energized, are
5 when I'm speeding somehow. Take, for example ... um ...
6 roller coasters! While my friends are scared to death on the
7 steep, downhill drops, I've got my arms in the air, and I'm
8 cheering my head off! That feeling of the wind whipping
9 past me ... it's like ... freedom!
10   Or what about sledding! Swooping past the trees!
11 Everything looks like stripes of color zipping by ... like
12 when the tracking needs adjusting on the VCR. You know?
13 Little bits of ice sting my face, but it doesn't really hurt. It's
14 so ... wild!
15   I want to try bungee jumping! Yeah! Or — or
16 whitewater rafting! Cool! Or — or skydiving!
17   The closest I get to that feeling of speed, these days, is
18 riding on my bike, but it's just not enough. Something's
19 missin'. It just doesn't make my heart pound, if you know
20 what I mean.
21   Whenever I ride without touching the handlebars or if I
22 pop a wheelie, my mom says I'm tempting fate. She won't
23 even let me buy a skateboard! Bummer. She says that in
24 order to enjoy life to its fullest, I've gotta slow down ...
25 *(Sigh) ... **Women!***
26
27
28
29
30

Romeo

1   All right! The director just posted the results of the
2 school auditions! I got the part of Romeo! Can you believe
3 it? Me! The lead! Just when my sister had me this close to
4 believing that I had no more chance of getting Romeo than
5 Edgar, the school dweeb, did — I'm not kidding — she
6 actually said, *(Mimics)* "You'll get the part of Romeo when
7 Dad buys me a Mercedes, which is never, Fool. Take a
8 good look at yourself!" Well, Sis, *(Taking a comb from left*
9 *rear pocket)* just look at me now. *(Combing)* Yup, prepare to
10 drive me to opening night in your brand new c—
11   Holy Smoke! Opening night! It's two months away!
12 How the heck am I supposed to learn all these lines in two
13 months? *(Takes script from right rear pocket.)* How will I ever
14 memorize all this? I'll be the laughing stock of the whole
15 school! I'll be kicked out of Drama Club! Just like in Act
16 III. Where is that part? *(Searches script.)* Yeah, here it is:
17
18   "Hence — banished is banished from the world,
19   And the world's exile is death. Then banished
20   Is death mistermed. Calling death 'banishment,'
21   Thou cut'st my head off with a golden ax
22   And smilest upon the stroke that murders me."
23   *(Romeo and Juliet, Act 3, Scene 3)*
24
25   You said it, William Shakespeare. I'm dead meat.
26
27
28
29
30

Con Artist

1   Good morning, Mrs. Jacobs. My, you're looking nice
2 today. Is that a new scarf? Oh thank you! Yes, I thought I'd
3 wear a tie today, in honor of our Parts of Speech quiz. And
4 may I add that I think an oral test is a great, really super
5 idea? Oh sure, Mrs. Jacobs, I know there are other
6 students in line. OK, I'm all set. Ask away!

7   An adverb? OK. I know this one. Adverb, adverb,
8 adverb. No, don't tell me. An adverb ... is a word that
9 describes ... a verb and ... a verb and ... Mrs. Jacobs, is
10 someone at the door? *(Waits for her to check, quickly flips his*
11 *tie up to read the answers written on the back, repositions his*
12 *tie, and smiles with an innocent look on his face.)* **I guess**
13 whoever it was changed his mind! Anyway, Mrs. Jacobs, an
14 adverb describes a verb, an adjective, or another adverb.
15 How's that? Go ahead, ask me another one!

16   An adjective? An adjective. Didn't you just ask me
17 adjective? Oh yeah, that was adverb. An adjective. Man, I
18 *know* this one. Ad-jec-tive ... Watch out, Mrs. Jacobs,
19 there's a huge spider on the back of your chair! *(As she*
20 *looks away, he does his "tie bit" once again.)* **Aw gee whiz, I**
21 think it made it out the window. Anyway, an adjective
22 describes a noun or pronoun.

23   Yup, I sure did, Mrs. Jacobs. I took your advice to heart
24 and studied really hard last night. Yup, you've been an
25 inspiration to me. You've changed my whole ... Send in the
26 next kid? Wow, that sure was easy, Mrs. Jacobs. Yes
27 Ma'am, I'll definitely keep studying my parts of speech! Yes
28 Ma'am, I *will* work hard! Beg your pardon? *(Sheepishly)* **Yes**
29 Ma'am, next time, I'll leave the tie at home.
30

Mr. Perfect

1   My little brother is heaven's gift to mankind. Oh yes.
2   Just ask my parents. Oh yes. He's the perfect child. Might
3   as well dub him a knight now — Why wait till he's older?
4   Hey, why not give him an honorary degree now to save
5   some time later? Yeah, how 'bout his picture on a postage
6   stamp? I know — What about sainthood?
7   Jealous? Me? Now, why should I be jealous? I should
8   be honored to live in the same house as our little prince.
9   After all, Mr. Perfect always gets good grades ... Mr.
10 Perfect is so cute and adorable ... Mr. Perfect's room is
11 always clean ... He even hugs and kisses and salivates all
12 over the relatives. Yes, I am lucky to share his genes.
13   Every now and then, I forget how blessed I am. Silly
14 me. Take yesterday for example: *someone* had taken my
15 baseball glove without even asking and left it outside in the
16 rain over night. But ... oh ... it was only an accident! Of
17 course! How dense of me not to realize that! Or last week
18 for example: Mr. Sunshine had left the top off of the trash
19 can, which was an open invitation to every raccoon in the
20 state. There was garbage all over the yard. But the little
21 angel makes mistakes because he's so young, you see. And
22 cleaning up the yard is a big job, too big for such a little guy
23 like my brother. So, of course it makes sense that I would
24 have to spend my Saturday scooping up old bones, rotten
25 fruit crawling with ants, used kitty litter ... of course!
26   I can't wait until Mr. Perfect moves up to my school
27 next year. Maybe he has my parents wrapped around his
28 obnoxious little finger ... but High School ... that's my
29 territory. *(Evil, suggestive laugh)*
30

Homework Excuses

1   **Shhh.** *(Looks left and right.)* **Step into my office, kid.**
2 **Make it fast and be sure to shut the boys' room door.**
3   **So ... you want to make use of my services, huh? OK,**
4 **here's my rates. Homework excuses: three for a dollar, six**
5 **for two dollars, or ten for three. That's a bargain — you**
6 **get one free! English compositions: two dollars a page.**
7 **Social studies time lines and maps: three bucks a pop.**
8 **Science projects: five bills each plus you pay for supplies.**
9 **So, what's your pleasure, m'boy?**
10   Ah ... the old homework scam. You got cash? No money
11 — no honey. No cash — you get trash. No moolah ... um ...
12 well, you get the point. Go for it; lay your coins on the sink,
13 my man. Ah-hah! Looks like you're goin' for six excuses for
14 two buck-er-oonies. OK ... gotta take out the ol' black book.
15 Got your pencil and paper ready? Good — start writing.
16   Numero uno: I really did my homework, but I left it in my
17 Dad's car, and he's on his way to Canada. Two: I worked all
18 night and then my baby brother threw up all over it. Three:
19 We just got a new puppy, and it chewed up the first page and
20 peed on the second. Four: I left it on the bus and the bus
21 driver gave it to her own kid who goes to a whole 'nother
22 school. Five: My grandma loved reading it so much that she
23 insisted on taking it to the old age home we dragged her to
24 this weekend. I tried to wrestle her for it, but she's a strong
25 one, my granny. And last but not least, number six: My uncle
26 works for the FBI, see, and he thought that the essay topic
27 was highly suspicious. He's checking the assignment
28 question for evidence of an international spy ring.
29   There. Did you get all that? Hope it helps, pal, and be
30 sure to mention my name to your friends. Good luck, kid!

Orangutan

1   Hi, Buddy! It's me — remember? Gotta nice apple here,
2   but I need to check if anyone's lookin'. OK. Coast's clear.
3   *(Pantomimes taking an apple out of his pocket and throwing it*
4   *into a cage.)* **Like that? Yeah, thought you would. Oops!**
5   *(Sees a passer-by and holds up a newspaper found on the bench*
6   *to block being seen.)*
7   **Whoa, close one! I'm supposed to be in school, y'see.**
8   **Today's oral report day in English class. We're expected to**
9   **get up and give a speech like we're the famous, dead guys**
10   **in our book reports. I can't ... I just can't. I've tried — it's**
11   **not like I haven't tried before ... but every time I stand up**
12   **in front of a class, I turn into ... somebody else. When I'm**
13   **up there, I feel all out of proportion. My arms feel like**
14   **they're so long that my knuckles could scrape the rug. My**
15   **legs feel so short that I'm sure everybody's thinking my**
16   **growth is stunted. I feel my eyes start to dart all over the**
17   **place, and I can't get my words out right. Instead of**
18   **making sense, I sound like I'm grunting!**
19   **No offense, guy, but ... that's what made me think of**
20   **you. I figured if anyone would understand, it'd be you. I**
21   **mean, not only do I look like you, but when I have to speak**
22   **in public, I feel all caged up ... just like you.**
23   **The only difference, though, is that *I* feel miserable.**
24   **Meanwhile, *you* ... you just swing around and have fun.**
25   **You seem to block everybody out. You just do your own**
26   **thing without worrying what everyone else is thinking.**
27   **Hey! That's it! Who cares about the other kids? I know**
28   **my speech inside and out! Just block 'em all out! Excuse**
29   **me, pal — I've got an oral report to give!**
30

Chipmunk Emergency

1   No Miss, I don't have an appointment, but I've gotta
2 see the vet right away! ... No, my dad's at work and my
3 mom's doing some food shopping. Please! This is an
4 emergency! ... Would you quit asking questions? I'll tell
5 you everything *after* you get this little guy in to see the vet!
6 Look, I think he's dying!
7   ... Oh, man, I don't believe this. What do you mean the
8 doctor only treats domestic animals? You mean dogs and
9 cats have more rights than wild animals do? That's ...
10 that's so unfair! It's prejudice — that's what it is! What
11 makes a guinea pig more important than a squirrel? Huh?
12 Look, that woman has a hamster in that cage! I've got a
13 little, weenie chipmunk! What's the difference? I have a
14 mind to go home, put my gerbil in a shoe box, put this
15 poor chipmunk in its cage, and call it a domestic pet! Only
16 by then it'd be dead, lady, and it'll be your fault!
17   ... Don't tell me to calm down. I'm responsible! Don't
18 you see? I ran over this little chipmunk with my bike, and
19 I've got to save it! I swear I didn't even see it! I felt this
20 horrible bump and heard the highest, most pitiful squeal
21 you can imagine. I'll probably hear that noise in my sleep
22 for the rest of my life!
23   Please Miss, every moment we argue is another minute
24 that the doctor could be using to treat this little guy. Who
25 would it hurt just to let me *talk* to the vet? Mrs. Hamster-
26 owner, would it bother you if I went ahead of you? Mr.
27 Man-with-the-poodle, can I please go first? See Lady? They
28 don't mind. Come on, I'm begging you. What have you got
29 to lose?
30

Mischief Night

1   If I do say so myself ... I am the King of Mischief Night.
2   Y'see the key word here is *mischief*. Now, some of my low
3   IQ friends confuse the word *mischief* with *vandalism*. But
4   if you want to hang with *me* the night before Halloween,
5   you gotta be cool, y'hear?
6   Graffiti is old news. Besides, why would anyone want
7   to paint trees and road signs all over town? Duh! We'd
8   have to look at that mess for the rest of the year. And
9   throwing eggs is lame. Somebody once smashed raw eggs
10   on my dad's car, and it literally took off the paint. Not
11   good. Peeking in people's windows? You could get your
12   butt arrested! Not smart.
13   Nah, the trick is to play little ... let's call them ...
14   pranks ... but not your ordinary practical jokes. They've
15   gotta have ... *style*. First we'll sneak a bag of cat litter into
16   the Jackson's doghouse. Then we can leave a note that
17   says, "Cats rule!" See? Style. The next step will be the
18   Fletcher's fish pond. I found an old fishing pole in the
19   dumpster. We can prop it up and hook on one of my
20   sister's paper dolls. Our message can say, "Revenge of the
21   Goldfish!" The best idea is to write a love letter on the
22   Home Ec teacher's driveway and sign it, "Love, Principal
23   Wyland." 'Course we'd write it with bars of soap. Hey,
24   clean and biodegradable, right?
25   So, what do you say? Partners?
26
27
28
29
30

Garage Sale

1   I'm rich! Nope — it wasn't the lottery. Uh-uh, no
2 relative died. No, not even the Prize Patrol. We just had a
3 garage sale!
4   When my mom roped us into cleaning out the attic, it
5 was bad enough. But then she turned into a spring
6 cleaning maniac! We had to clear out the basement,
7 closets, even under beds! So there we were with a garage
8 full of junk. Dad nearly croaked when he figured how much
9 it would cost us in garbage stickers. Out of the blue my
10 little sister piped in, "I know! Leth have a garage thale!"
11 How do kids come up with these things?
12   So, this morning was the big day. As soon as the clock
13 hit nine, people swarmed onto our property like termites
14 on wood. All our worthless trash somehow turned into
15 antiques and collectibles overnight! It was like a scene
16 from a science fiction movie! Old ladies were diving for toy
17 cars! Little kids — tripping each other to get to the stuffed
18 animals! Grown women — bidding on Barbies! Sports
19 equipment was like silver! Baseball cards were like gold!
20 Either these people knew something we didn't know, or
21 else they were totally bonkers!
22   But I'm not complaining! I just made over fifty dollars
23 ... with junk! I'm rich! God bless America!
24
25
26
27
28
29
30

Teacher Horror

1   Mom! Dad! You don't understand! It's not *me*! It's
2   them! How do you expect me to learn from a pack of
3   teachers who are more terrifying than anything I've ever
4   seen in horror movies?

5   I'm *not* exaggerating. This isn't the old days when
6   kindly teachers led kids down the path of learning, Mom —
7   oh, no. My day begins with Mrs. Epstein who I'm willing to
8   bet is the long-lost daughter of Frankenstein himself!
9   How's a guy supposed to concentrate with a giant, hulking
10   creature stomping around the room? She's got an ugly
11   brown wart on each side of her forehead which would
12   probably electrocute anybody who touched it. I *try* to focus
13   on my creative writing, but all I can do is stare at those
14   warts, waiting for bolts of lightning to zap out of them.

15   Science class is even worse! Who would name their son
16   Mr. Blood anyway? And tell me it's an accident that he
17   wears mostly black. Ever notice how white and pasty his
18   skin looks? Dad, whenever I'm working on a lab, Mr. Blood
19   swoops over to my desk and hovers behind me. Once from
20   the corner of my eye, I swear I saw him licking his lips!

21   Oh, and don't get me started on social studies. Is it
22   normal for a woman to have that much facial hair? What
23   about math — the teacher has the biggest eyes I've ever
24   seen ... set really far apart ... and they bug out like an
25   insect's! And French class —

26   *(Listens with a look or horror)* No Mom! No Dad! Not that!
27   What do you mean you're banning me from late night TV?
28   This is so unfair! Why is it you never, ever take my side?
29   Man, those teachers are even more powerful than I
30   thought.

Circus

1   Uh ... are you the manager? Oh good. Um ... I was
2 wondering how I go about joining your circus ... What? ...
3 Uh, h ... how old do I have to be? Oh well, that's perfect
4 'cause I just turned eighteen *today* as a matter of fact.
5 Yeah, I know I look way younger. I guess when I'm fifty, I'll
6 appreciate it, right? Ha-ha! *(Unconvincing laugh)*
7   So ... uh ... have you got any openings? I'm really wiry!
8 You could train me for the tightrope or the trapeze in no
9 time! I ... I'm great with animals! Horses ... lions ...
10 elephants? They're all pussycats to me! And strong, too —
11 I'm wiry but strong! Start me on the weights and I could
12 stand in for your strong man whenever you needed me! A
13 clown, yeah, I could be a clown! Look — you're smiling
14 already! Slap on the grease paint and shoot me outta a
15 cannon if you want! Heck, I'd even learn to eat fire! ...
16 Please?
17   What? ... Well, OK, I'm not exactly eighteen. Would you
18 believe sixteen? Thirteen? Oh man, this isn't gonna work.
19 Buy hey, it was worth a try wasn't it? Ha-ha-ha. *(Another*
20 *unconvincing laugh)*
21   Yeah, I just thought that I'd really fit in here. You guys
22 live such exciting lives: The action! The costumes! The
23 danger! Me? My life consists of homework ... the
24 orthodontist ... and taking out the garbage.
25   OK well ... thanks anyway ... and if you get an opening
26 in, say, five or six years ... here's my number.
27
28
29
30

Initiation

1   I think the moment of truth happens the instant when
2 what had once seemed like the greatest challenge known
3 to a guy like me becomes the stupidest, most insane idea
4 in the universe! OK spirits, I've had my moment! My eyes
5 are opened! I can go home, now! ... The only problem is ...
6 I haven't the foggiest clue where home is!
7   What kind of moron lets himself be blindfolded and
8 dragged to some creepy cemetery ... where he has to
9 spend the night ... alone? And why? To be one of the cool
10 guys! To be a man! To prove himself! What kind of half-wit
11 agrees to this kind of humiliation? *Me!* That's who!
12   The whole time I was stumbling through the woods,
13 with that dumb scarf over my eyes, I just kept thinking, "I
14 am so lucky. Every guy in school will be incredibly jealous.
15 Imagine me — given the chance to be one of the main men.
16 Me ... a member of the in-crowd! Me ... a step above
17 everyone else."
18   But now that I'm freezing my fanny off ... sitting in a
19 field of tombstones ... waiting for zombies to eat me alive
20 ... I feel like a world-class dweeb!
21   I gotta give the gang some credit, though. If they
22 hadn't talked me into this initiation — and if I hadn't been
23 jerk enough to go along with it — I would never have
24 realized what a farce this is. I'm like a cartoon character
25 whose light bulb just turned on. OK, so it's not a total loss.
26 But if I see a single body part that's not attached to a living
27 person ... I'm gonna wet myself!
28
29
30

Bathroom Blues

1   *(The actor uses two focal points in this monolog. The first is*
2   *the bathroom door, real or pantomimed, behind which is his*
3   *sister. The second is the audience which will be indicated as an*
4   *aside. He begins by banging on the door.)*
5   **Come on, Iris, you've been in there for thirty minutes**
6   **already. There are *other* people in this house, you know.**
7   **Did you fall in? No human needs the bathroom for half-a-**
8   **freakin' hour, Iris! Open the door before I bust it in!**
9   *(Aside)* **You know the definition of torture? It's being a**
10   **fraternal twin! Oh yeah, at first it's great. You get to share**
11   **a stroller, share a crib, wear similar clothes ... but then**
12   **you grow up and you're forced to share the same**
13   **bathroom!**
14   **Iris! I'm not kidding! Get your lazy butt outta there!**
15   **Stop staring in the mirror — you'll make it crack! All that**
16   **makeup won't fix *your* face — it's a lost cause! And quit**
17   **putting on all that smelly junk! Bees are swarming all**
18   **around the bathroom door looking for the flower garden!**
19   **Iris, the school bus is due in twenty minutes. Lemme in!**
20   *(Aside)* **She's been like this ever since Scott Kingsley**
21   **started sending her those stupid notes in homeroom.**
22   **That's another pain about being a twin. You grow up with**
23   **the exact same friends ... all hangin' out together ...**
24   **swimming, biking, playing ball. And then you wake up one**
25   **morning, and your best friend has a crush on your twin**
26   **sister! How gross is that?**
27   **Iris, I swear on my life, if you don't get out of the**
28   **bathroom this minute, I'm gonna tell Scott Kingsley how**
29   **you still sleep with your teddy bear! I'm giving you a count**
30   **of three. One! ... Two! ... Three! Iris!**

1   *(Aside)* **The other problem with being a fraternal twin**
2 **is that she always knows when I'm bluffing.** *(Sits on the*
3 *floor, head in hands.)*
4
5
6
7
8
9
10
11
12
13
14
15
16
17
18
19
20
21
22
23
24
25
26
27
28
29
30
31
32
33
34
35

Lady Doctor

1   Oh ... where's Dr. Morton? No offense, but I've been
2 seeing Dr. Morton ever since I was born and ... Excuse me?
3 ... Oh, you're his new partner? ... Um ... nice to meet you,
4 Dr. Lady ... I ... I mean, Dr. Lacey.
5   But ... uh ... you see, Doctor, like I was saying ... um ...
6 Dr. Morton always gives me my check-ups and ... What? ...
7 What do you mean he's on vacation? Why doesn't he go
8 away during the summer like everyone else? ... Well, isn't
9 that just great! Here I've finally gotten over my fear of
10 taking off my clothes in front of that little old man ... and
11 he goes away to some tropical island somewhere!
12 Meanwhile, I'm wearing a silly paper dress ... in front of a
13 strange woman!
14   ... Huh? No, of course I don't want my mother in here.
15 What do I look like — a kid? No, I'll be fine. I just need to
16 calm down, that's all.
17   I know, I'll just pretend that you're Dr. Morton. Yeah,
18 that's a good idea. I'll just shut my eyes and visualize a
19 short, chubby man *(Shuts eyes)* with a gray beard and bushy
20 eyebrows. OK, I think this is working. Now I'll just take a
21 deep breath ... Dr. Morton, that's a really pretty perfume
22 you're wearing — *(Eyes pop open.)* Oh man!
23   I'm sorry, Doctor, but this just isn't going to work.
24 Nothing personal, Doc, but you're a woman! ... Yeah, I
25 guess you knew that.
26
27
28
29
30

Plane Ride

1 (The actor has a look of sheer terror on his face. He is
2 clutching the edges of his seat. His focus is to his side as if to a
3 passenger beside him.)
4   Huh? Oh, no — I'm fine. A-OK. Happy as a clam. Cool
5 as a breeze. Relaxed as ... as ... How come we're rolling?
6 I thought planes were supposed to fly! Holy cow!
7   ... (Weak laugh) Heh-heh, oh, so you noticed? Yeah, this
8 is my first flight. My older brother and his new wife just
9 moved down south. Invited me for a visit. Yeah, thought I'd
10 say good-bye to the snow 'n' ice for a week. Pretty great
11 opportunity. Yeah, I ... Holy moly, we're speeding up!
12   Oh man! Oh man! The skin on my face is pushing back
13 toward my ears! How the heck can the pilot see the other
14 planes on the roadway when he's driving this fast? I'm too
15 young to die! Holy mackerel, we're heading up! My ears —
16 the pressure's too great! They're gonna pop! They ... they ...
17   What happened? (Moving jaw to relax his ears) This is
18 much better. Ears are back to normal ... Skin has returned
19 to my face ... What happened? (Listens to passenger.) The
20 window? Well, OK. (Looks out.) Holy macaroni! We're
21 flying! Look how far up we are! I can barely make out the
22 trees anymore. My brother's right — the clouds really do
23 look like cotton candy. Can you believe it? This is great!
24 Lookit the ocean! It's a sheet of blue! This is the most
25 exciting moment I've ever experienced!
26   This deserves a celebration. Stewardess! Stewardess!
27 Yes, a Coke, please ... and one for my friend over here.
28 Heck, let's make it a party! Cokes for *everybody!*
29
30

Attitude

1   *(Doing push-ups)* **Twenty-three … twenty-four …** *(Groan)*
2   **twenty-five! OK, now for the sit-ups. Great for the abs!**
3   *(Starts sit-ups.)* **One … two … th, th, th, three … f, f, f, for**
4   **… get it!** *(Panting)* **No more. No way. No how! The mind is**
5   **willing, but the body is pooped!**
6   **How do those guys do it? You know the ones I mean:**
7   **those guys on TV with arms like boulders … chests like**
8   **barrels … frying pan stomachs … legs like tree trunks. I**
9   **want to be an Atlas! A stallion! A babe-magnet!**
10   **And no one can say I'm not trying! But … after a month**
11   **of working out every single day … the most that's**
12   **happened is that I lost a pound and maybe grew another**
13   **hair on my chin.**
14   **What am I doing wrong? It sure as heck can't be my**
15   **diet. I've drunk so many protein shakes that one of the**
16   **bathroom stalls in school has my name on it! And if I**
17   **swallow one more raw egg, I'm gonna barf up a lung!**
18   **I know … I know … you were about to tell me that**
19   **muscles don't matter. It's all in the attitude. Attitude? I** *got*
20   **attitude! The problem is that nobody takes attitude**
21   **seriously when it walks on chicken legs and talks with a**
22   **voice that cracks without warning!**
23   **Nope, the trick is, I gotta keep pluggin'. No pain — no**
24   **gain. I'm gonna exercise** *twice* **a day if I have to. And**
25   **someday … someday when reporters ask me what I did to**
26   **get such a manly physique … I'll toss my thick hair, flex my**
27   **awesome biceps, and say, "It's all in the** *attitude***, my**
28   **friend."**
29
30

Psychic Signals

1   Ray and I are bummin' around, same ol', same ol', and
2 it's getting to be a big drag. We do the same ol' things
3 every weekend: ride bikes, hang out at the pizza place ...
4 how much TV can two guys take? So, we start busting our
5 skulls thinking of something new to do ... when Ray sees
6 his Dad's wallet on the kitchen table.
7   Ray says, "Hey dude, check it out! Credit card!" So we
8 start brainstorming again. The mall is too far away — what
9 the heck could we do with a credit card out in Nowheres-
10 ville? That's when Ray blurts out, "Psychic Signals!" Aw,
11 come on, you know what I mean. It's one of those places
12 you call on the telephone and they, like, predict the future.
13 All you need is to be eighteen and have a credit card. Well,
14 *voila!* Ray can make his voice go really low and sound just
15 like his dad's!
16   So we get this lady with a really sexy voice, but we're
17 laughing, y'know, 'cause she's probably some eighty-year-
18 old woman the size of a tank. She starts to tell us all this
19 wild stuff like how many kids we're gonna have, if we'll be
20 healthy ... and then she says, "And at the end of the month
21 your father will open up his bills, scream bloody murder,
22 and make you pay him nineteen dollars and ninety-five
23 cents."
24   How the heck did she know that? That Psychic Signals
25 lady knew *exactly* what was going to happen, word for
26 word, down to the exact penny! It's amazing what the
27 human mind can do.
28
29
30

Poetry

1   This has to be the fruitiest homework assignment ever.
2 If my grade wasn't so borderline, I'd skip it. Where'd Mr.
3 Styles come up with the idea of writing a poem about an
4 interesting future career? How do I even begin? Oh man, I
5 stink at this stuff! *(Reads as he writes.)*
6   "I want to be a forest ranger." If he makes me read this
7 out loud, I'm making a bee-line for the door.
8   "I like it 'cause it offers danger." Well, it rhymes anyway!
9   "I'm at my best when I'm outside," What goes with
10 side? Ride? Hide? Glide?
11   "Watching deer that prance and birds that glide." Not
12 bad! I think I'm on a roll!
13   "I want to protect our streams and forests." No way,
14 Dummy. Nothing rhymes with forests. *(Crosses out the line.)*
15   "I want to protect our forests and streams." This way's
16 much better.
17   "For nature's gifts are wildlife's dreams." Aw, I dunno.
18 Maybe that's too sappy. Geez, I hate poetry.
19   "It's not about salary that I care."
20   "I just want to meet Smokey Bear!" *(Long peal of*
21 *laughter)* No, I can't. I'm tempted ... but I can't. Well, why
22 not? It's a poem, isn't it? There's nothing in the directions
23 that says I can't use humor. Yeah! I just dare that Mr.
24 Styles to flunk me for writing comedy. Yeah! ... Oh man ...
25 I hope I pass.
26
27
28
29
30

Takeover

1   Help! I'm outnumbered! I'm in a family of six and only
2   two of us are guys! Dad doesn't really count, though,
3   'cause he's always flying halfway around the world. He
4   doesn't know the true effects of ... *(Makes bugle noise)* **Tat-**
5   **dada-da** ... The Female Takeover!
6   They're controlling the world! I wake up to the sound
7   of girl bands blasting on the stereo. I go into the bathroom
8   ... Stockings hang from the shower curtain rod ... The top
9   of the sink is lined with potions and lotions ... I trip over
10   pink, furry slippers!
11   I stumble to the refrigerator. Food takes my mind off
12   anything. All I can find are fruits, sprouts, little sandwiches
13   with the crust cut off, flavored teas ... quiche! *Argh!* *(Or*
14   *similar outburst of frustration)* **Give me meat!**
15   Dazed, I make my way toward the television. Rats! One
16   of ... *them* ... has gotten there ahead of me. She's
17   watching a lovey-dovey, mushy-gushy, smoochie-poo show
18   again. I cover my eyes so I don't go blind! What's wrong
19   with war movies? Action thrillers? Horror flicks?
20   These females are taking away my personal freedom. I
21   want to put my feet up on the table without knocking over
22   an open bottle of nail polish! I dream of scratching myself
23   without hearing a chorus of giggles! I beg to burp out loud!
24   Men! We must join forces! Band together! Unite! It's
25   time to rise up and face the enemy! Fight now or forever
26   regret the day of ... *(Bugle noise)* **Tat-dada-da!** The Female
27   Takeover!
28
29
30

Monologs
for Girls
(Serious)

Two-Faced

1   I hate her! What makes Leslie so popular? She's so
2 rotten to me, and I've never done anything to deserve it! I
3 do my work ... I hang out with my friends ... I never even
4 say two words to her. But every day if I happen to walk
5 past her — just to sharpen my pencil or something like that
6 — she has to make some annoying sound or just insult me.
7 She makes disgusting throw-up noises, not loud enough
8 for the teacher to hear, but just enough to make me
9 nervous ... or she'll whisper something like, "What's that
10 on your shirt?" Then I worry all day about what I might
11 have stuck to me.
12   The worst part is that everyone knows what she's like.
13 When she's not around everybody says, "That Leslie, she's
14 such a jerk" or "Leslie can be so mean!" But as soon as she
15 walks into the room, it's like all the kids are hypnotized or
16 something! The same people who just talked behind her
17 back start kissing her feet! Not really. You know what I
18 mean. They start saying, "Hey Leslie, would you like my
19 extra candy bar?" or "Oh Leslie, there's an extra seat near
20 me!" It gets me so mad! I think I'm angrier at my friends
21 for being so two-faced, than I am at Leslie for being such
22 a pain!
23   I don't care what Leslie says or why she's decided that
24 I'm not good enough for her! I'm going to be one way
25 behind her back and the same way in front of her. That's
26 the way I am, and that's the way I'm going to stay!
27
28
29
30

Caught

1   What if he calls my mother? This'll kill her! Think! How
2 can I talk my way out of this one? OK, just calm down.
3 When that dorky cashier comes back in with the cop, I'll
4 just say that it was all an accident. Yeah, that's good. Let's
5 try it out.
6   *(Pretending to cry)* "Oh, Mr. Policeman, Sir, I was
7 carrying so many books and there was nowhere to put
8 them down! So *(Sniffle)* I figured that I'd put the pen in my
9 pocket while I reached for my money. Of course I was
10 planning to pay for it! I would never, ever, never, ever, ever,
11 ever try to steal anything!" Hey, not bad! I bet they'll fall
12 for that one in less than a minute.
13   *(Looks around the room impatiently and awkwardly.)* **Where**
14 the heck are they, anyway? I hate being all alone. It's kind
15 of scary. Man, if I had known there was a hidden camera,
16 I never would have taken that stupid pen. I didn't even
17 need the dumb thing. It's just that it looked so sparkly, like
18 a glittering rainbow. Who the heck cares anyway? I mean,
19 the store has tons of pens and makes lots of money. What
20 is the big deal over one eency-weency pen, anyway? It's not
21 like I hurt anyone.
22   Mom'll be hurt, though. She'll be so embarrassed ...
23 and disappointed ... and ... miserable. Oh, why did I take
24 that stinking pen anyway? I feel like the biggest idiot in the
25 world ... the biggest idiot in the whole entire world!
26
27
28
29
30

Starlight

1   Star light, star bright, first star I see tonight, I wish I
2 may, I wish I might, have this wish I wish tonight. I wish ...
3 I wish I were beautiful!
4   Oh, I know, Starlight. You're thinking that I'm cute
5 enough already. But I'm tired of being cute. Cute is for
6 cuddly puppies ... and cooing babies ... and yellow chicks.
7 Pollyanna was cute. *(Makes a disdainful face.)* Shirley Temple
8 was ... nauseating, actually. See what I mean? And those
9 cutesy-pie twins who are so popular make me want to pour
10 glue in their shorts. Cute is for losers — I want to be
11 beautiful!
12   I want to walk down the hallway in school and have all
13 the boys trip on their tongues. The girls would be so
14 jealous that their eyes would pop out of their heads and
15 bob around on little coiled springs. The teachers would be
16 so awestruck that they'd lose their grade books, and
17 everybody would have to get A's! *(Giggle)*
18   I want to walk home from school and hear the screech
19 of tires as drivers passing me suddenly put on their brakes
20 for a better look! I want to go to a restaurant and hear the
21 crash of dishes as waiters pass out having taken one peek
22 at me! I want to go to the beach and see the lifeguards
23 stumble over one another to see who gets to give me CPR!
24   *(Sigh)* Oh OK, Starlight. I know it's a pretty unrealistic
25 wish ... but a girl can dream, can't she?
26
27
28
29
30

Doodling in Class

1   Uh ... hello? Mr. Mapleton? Uh, yes, well ... uh ... Mrs.
2 Troad sent me ... a message, Sir? ... Uh, no ... it's more for
3 ... discipline.
4   No Sir, you probably haven't ever seen me before ...
5 I'm not that noticeable.
6   ... My name? Oh, I'm Wendy Trumbel ... Oh thank you,
7 I think I *will* sit down. I'm kind of ... well, I've never been
8 in trouble before, and I'm a little shaky. I know I was
9 wrong, Sir. Do whatever you have to do. Call my parents.
10 Schedule me for detention. I'd be really good at scrubbing
11 desks. Go ahead, *(Deep breath)* I can take it!
12   What? Oh, well, whenever Mrs. Troad starts screaming
13 at the class ... well ... I used to get kind of watery ... but ...
14 I found that drawing quietly until she was finished made
15 me ... feel better. It's not a bad thing, really, because ... um
16 ... I've gotten pretty good at expressing myself, this year. I
17 guess you've noticed that I'm ... sort of ... shy, but
18 sketching in this note pad has really become kind of a ...
19 release for me. I've been able to ... uh ... put some of my
20 feelings on paper. It helps, really.
21   *(Referring to note pad)* See, this snake is Mrs. Troad, and
22 she's calling the rabbit "stupid." The rabbit is supposed to
23 look like James, but I'm not that great an artist. I felt much
24 calmer after I drew that one, though. Uh ... and this one is
25 a tiger. It's supposed to be Mrs. Troad ripping up
26 Amanda's test when she couldn't remember the date that
27 the Constitution was written. Um ... and see this puddle?
28 That's how Zach felt when Mrs. Troad told the class that
29 he'd have to go to summer school ... Today, Sir? Well,
30 today she was yelling at *everybody*. I guess we didn't do

1   well on the Current Events essays. I didn't even realize
2   that she was looking over my shoulder ... Yes Sir, it *is*
3   another picture of Mrs. Troad ... Yes Sir, she *is* chewing
4   up a bunch of students. That pile on the floor — those
5   are the kids she spit out. I'm sorry, Mr. Mapleton.
6   What? Oh no, Sir. I'll never doodle in class again! ...
7   That's it? ... That's my whole punishment? ... But Sir,
8   Mrs. Troad said that I was in a ton of trouble. *(Listens.)*
9   Yes Sir, I'll tell her you want to see her immediately after
10 class. Thanks, Mr. Mapleton!
11
12
13
14
15
16
17
18
19
20
21
22
23
24
25
26
27
28
29
30
31
32
33
34
35

Traitor

1   How could you treat me that way? No, I'm serious. My
2 mom always tells me to put myself in the other person's
3 shoes. But what I don't get is — how can a person, a
4 human being with feelings and a heart, hurt somebody so
5 badly? How can you live with yourself? Don't you make
6 yourself sick?
7   ... I've never had a best friend before. Well, not like the
8 way we were, anyway. Sure, I had lots of buddies ...
9 playmates ... pals. But you are the first person who I really
10 opened up to. I trusted you. I told you things I've never
11 even told my mom ... my inner-most thoughts ... my
12 deepest secrets. I thought ... I honestly thought ... that we
13 were closer than sisters ... friends for life. We were like ...
14 the same mind in two people. You know?
15   No, of course you don't — because if you had felt those
16 things, you would never have blabbed my secrets to
17 Ashley. I was so embarrassed! What about trust? What
18 about privacy? What about friendship? How dare you! How
19 dare you take my personal secrets and spread them to the
20 first popular girl who bothers to talk to you for more than
21 two minutes!
22   How does it feel? Huh? Do you feel cool now? Are you
23 with-it? One of the in-crowd? Or do you feel like a dirty,
24 back-stabbing, traitor — which you *should* 'cause that's
25 exactly what you *are*!
26
27
28
29
30

The Tie

1   Yes, Sir ... um ... Could you tell me how much that tie
2 is? ... That much? Oh no, Sir, I didn't mean anything by it
3 ... I just ... well ... This is all I've got.
4   Do you think ... maybe ... you'd have some sort of
5 chores around here? I'm a really hard worker. I can fold
6 clothes ... gift-wrap ... unpack boxes ... I can do anything
7 you need! Maybe I can *earn* the money for that tie! You
8 see, I'd really like to get my Dad something special for
9 Father's Day. He's been so busy since Mom ... well, she's
10 not really around much. And Dad's been doing everything
11 all by himself ... making supper, laundry, you know. So, do
12 you think that maybe you could — What? ... um, no, Sir. I
13 don't think I'm old enough for working papers ...
14   Hey, what if I worked real cheap? I mean, you wouldn't
15 have to pay me near what you pay ... say, that high school
16 kid who's working behind the cash register. It'd be a
17 bargain, really! You could pay me by the foot! I'm at least
18 a foot shorter than he is, so you could pay me a whole buck
19 or two less than you pay him!
20   I've *gotta* get that tie, Mister! My Daddy's always
21 buying me things that he says will make me feel pretty.
22 Now *I* want to get *him* something to make him feel ... well
23 ... handsome. Isn't there anything I can do? Take out the
24 garbage? Clean the restroom?
25   No Sir, I didn't know that you're having a sale
26 tomorrow. I ... uh ... didn't see any sign. This tie? You'll
27 hold it for me? But, this is all the money I've saved and ...
28 It's enough? ... um ... Mister? ... Do you have a daughter
29 at home? ... Yup, thought so. *(Smile)*
30

73

Alcoholic

1   (Nervously) I've got this friend, see ... You wouldn't
2   know her ... and she's kinda worried that ... that she's
3   gonna get hurt ... real bad. Yeah ... well ... and in health
4   class the movie said that if ... um ... someone needs help
5   — health help — that we're supposed to talk to an adult.
6   But ya see, this friend of mine ... well, she can't really talk
7   to her mom about it because ... well, that's the problem ...
8   it's ... uh ... her mom. I was — she was — um, actually *we*
9   ... were sorta hoping that you'd be able to help ... sorta.
10   We figured that I could ask you about it, and then I could
11   go tell my friend what I found out ... if that's OK with you.
12   ... I don't know where to begin ... It's kind of
13   embarrassing ... you know ... talking to someone I don't
14   know that well. (Deep breath) OK, here it is ... My friend's
15   mom has been majorly upset ever since my friend's dad
16   died. It was a car accident. I guess the mom feels guilty
17   because ... well, she was driving. And ... and when she gets
18   all upset like that ... she starts to drink a lot ... and when
19   she gets all drunk, she turns into a whole 'nother person!
20   She yells and hits and curses and kicks and ... and ... and
21   my friend, she doesn't know what to do! She doesn't want
22   to get her mom into any kind of trouble ... but ... but she's
23   afraid. She's scared to eat. She's too petrified to sleep.
24   And ... and up till now, she's been too frightened to tell
25   anybody about it!
26   ... So, if you could ... like ... tell me what to do ... I'll
27   go and tell my friend. I — she — *we*'d really appreciate it.
28
29
30

Gymnastics

1   Gymnastics rules! I don't get all the talk about drinking
2 or drugs. What's the big appeal? You want to relax? You
3 want to forget all your problems? Come with me to my
4 gymnastics class! Listen to me — I sound like a gymnastics
5 junkie! But honestly, it's true.
6   You can feel the difference the second you walk into
7 the gym. It's like a beehive of activity. To the left are girls
8 swinging on bars of all heights. Girls fly through the air
9 from one pole to the next. There's always that scary thrill:
10 What if someone falls? But no one ever does.
11   Behind them girls are leap-frogging over leather
12 horses. Further back others are doing somersaults,
13 cartwheels, flips! Little girls, big girls, skinny ones, fat ...
14 and not a one standing still ... all moving in a happy frenzy!
15   To the right are the trampolines. Girls are jumping!
16 Spinning! Doing acrobatics in mid-air! Not to mention the
17 obstacle course, and the rope climb and ... and ... oh, and
18 the noise! Your ears fill with a high-pitched buzz of
19 laughter and squeals! I'm telling you there's nothing like it!
20   And who cares if you goof up every now and then? It's
21 funny, actually. Everybody laughs and then cheers you on
22 to try again! And when you make it ... when you soar
23 through the air and land, smack down on two feet ...
24 there's such a feeling of ... of "Oh yeah — I'm cool!"
25   The only thing *I* can't understand is — how come
26 everybody hasn't caught onto this natural high? It's ...
27 awesome!
28
29
30

Prejudice

1   Sometimes my friends, my so-called friends I should
2 say, can be such ... such ... *urgh!* If I said what I want to
3 call them, I'd be as bad as they are! But think of the worst
4 word you're not allowed to say ... and that's how my
5 friends acted today.

6   They are so prejudiced sometimes! And they're so
7 weird — I mean, it's not the typical racism you'd expect
8 from such jerks ... it's weight. How ridiculous is that? ...
9 Not that any kind of prejudice makes sense. It's not like we
10 live in the Dark Ages. But I have to admit that this weight
11 thing surprises me. And the strangest part? Not only are
12 my friends mean to Alicia ... but they've been nasty to *me*
13 for hanging out with her!

14   OK, I do wish Alicia cared more about staying in shape
15 ... not because of the look thing ... but ... well, I just worry
16 about her, that's all. I know gym class is really hard for her,
17 and I don't want her to give up because ... because she's
18 totally cool and I don't want her to throw away her health.
19 You know?

20   But that's no reason to say cutting remarks to her.
21 That's no reason to call her names! On Alicia's *meanest*
22 day, she'd never be as rotten as my so-called friends were
23 today! And to call *me* names for liking one of the nicest
24 girls in school? Well, that one just blows my mind!

25   I think my mom's right. I think it's that time in my life
26 to decide who's a real friend and who's a ... a ... big ... a
27 big ... Oh, *you* know the word I'm thinking!
28
29
30

Parent Trouble

1   Mom? Dad? Sit down. No, don't talk. For once, just
2 once, let me do the talking! I'm sick of all this arguing and
3 ... and I'm not going to take it anymore!
4   Don't you two realize what all this yelling does to me?
5 It's not good enough that you send me out of the room. It
6 makes you feel like responsible parents, but that's all it
7 does. I have ears, you know. When you guys start
8 screaming at each other, nothing helps. It's not like I'm
9 eavesdropping. I shut my door ... I blast my stereo ... I
10 bury my head under my stuffed animals ... but it doesn't
11 help! It sounds like you're in the same room with me!
12   And the things you say to each other ... If *I* ever said
13 anything *close* to those things, I'd be grounded for life! So
14 how come you two can say them? The things you two call
15 each other should be saved for really bad people like
16 thieves or murderers! So why do you say them to each
17 other? Why would you say those things to somebody you
18 love? You keep telling me you love each other ... but how
19 am I supposed to believe that? And if I can't trust that my
20 parents tell me the truth ... well then, how ... how can I
21 believe *anything* anymore? ... Huh? ... Huh? ... Go ahead,
22 I'm waiting.
23
24
25
26
27
28
29
30

Camp

1   *(Mimicking)* "Go to the cabin and think about it." What
2   am I — a baby? What is this — like the time-out corner in
3   nursery school? Yeah, I'll think about it all right. Think-
4   schmink! All I did was short-sheet Suzy's cot. I mean, this
5   is camp — it's expected, right? And OK, so I put petroleum
6   jelly on the toilet seat. How was I supposed to know
7   Amanda would slide off and chip a tooth? Geez, what a
8   klutz! And I'm telling you I had no clue that when I sewed
9   up the bottoms of the counselor's jeans, she'd wham her
10   foot in that hard. Frankly, I don't believe she needs crutches
11   just for a broken big toe. I think it's a sympathy scam.
12   That dumb camp director thinks he's so ...
13   intimidating: "Just go to the cabin and think about it."
14   What — does he expect me to cry or something? I was just
15   goin' for laughs. That guy has no sense of humor. I bet he
16   was the kid with his underwear up the flagpole when *he*
17   was a camper. That's what my dad did when he was my
18   age. He sneaked into his bunkmate's trunk, swiped a pair
19   of underpants — only when Dad tells it, he calls them
20   "gatchies" — and hoisted them up the flagpole. What a
21   riot! I learned the greatest pranks from that dad of mine!
22   I bet *he'd* understand if he were here. Not like that stick-
23   in-the-mud camp director.
24   Hey, what's all that noise? *(Runs to window.)* Seems to be
25   coming from in front of the mess hall! What's everybody
26   laughing about? Oh look, they're pointing. Something's up
27   the flagpole. That's strange. It kinda looks like the top of a
28   two-piece bathing suit. Wait a minute! I have one just like ...
29   *(Running off angrily)* **Very funny, you guys!**
30

The Big D

1   *(Calling out the door)* **Bye! Have a good time! Don't stay**
2   out too late!
3   Talk about role reversal! Mom's going out on her first
4   date since the big D. You know, D-I-V-O-R-C-E. It's a dirty
5   word in this house. Never say that word in front of my
6   mother if you know what's good for you! Anyway, she met
7   this guy at work, and I finally convinced her to go out with
8   him. Isn't that upside-down? I had to talk her into going
9   out with a man! Blows my mind!
10   I hope it works, too. Maybe then I'll get my mom back.
11   I know that sounds weird. I mean, I've always had my
12   mom, really ... but she's been a whole other person since
13   the big D. I used to have a mother who always told me
14   what to do ... always knew the right thing to say ... could
15   solve any problem ... and ... and I felt like she was a
16   hundred years older and wiser than I was.
17   Now, she wants to be my friend. My friend! Like she's
18   my age or something! She's been dressing like me! Talking
19   like me! Watching my TV shows with me! Wearing all the
20   little doo-dads in her hair! Totally bizarre!
21   I'm kinda hoping that if she has fun on her date and
22   *likes* this guy, that ... well ... that she'll settle down a little
23   bit. Maybe she'll forget about being my friend and ... and
24   start acting her age. Moms! They sure wear a kid down.
25
26
27
28
29
30

Myths

1   I think it's a *sin* to lie to kids. And don't tell me the
2 story about how *(Mocking)* "Sometimes the truth needs to
3 be interpreted in a *special* way for young minds!" Baloney!
4 Or how 'bout this one? "White lies are used to protect a
5 child's feelings." Give it a rest. I've heard it all.
6   There oughta be a *fine*, some penalty for parents who
7 out 'n' out lie to their kids. Maybe then they'd think twice
8 before they come out with messages that their kids believe
9 ... things that'll break their hearts someday. Didn't you
10 ever see a kid howling because she learned that the Easter
11 Bunny is a big, fat fib? Haven't you ever met someone who
12 hates Christmas after she found out that there is no Santa
13 Claus?
14   And it's not just lies to *little* kids that annoy the heck
15 outta me. Parents twist the truth your whole life. How
16 about the famous myth that goes, "If you try hard enough,
17 you can do anything." What kind of a fairy tale is that? If
18 that were true, then explain how I can study math every
19 single night, go for extra help twice a week, meet with a
20 high school math whiz for tutoring before every major test
21 ... and I still *bomb* at math! I'm waiting for the miracle. I'm
22 trying really hard, so when am I going to wake up with the
23 instant ability to ace my math tests? When do I turn into
24 the Human Calculator?
25   Hmph *(Or similar sigh)* ... do me a favor. Next time you
26 get the urge to water down ... whitewash ... or stretch the
27 truth, just try telling it like it is. I can take it.
28
29
30

Just a Kid

1   I just wanna be treated like a kid. That's funny 'cause
2 all my friends wanna be treated like adults. They don't
3 know how good they've got it.
4   In a way it's nice to be needed, I guess ... but there has
5 to be a limit, you know? I want some time to do my own
6 thing, some time for *me*. I tried telling Mom, but all she
7 said was, "I know it can be hard on you, honey, but in a
8 family this large, everyone needs to pitch in." She's right
9 — I know that. But it seems like ... well, since I'm the
10 oldest ... everybody expects me to be Miss Responsible ...
11 Miss Second Mom ... Miss You-don't-count-because-you're-
12 the-oldest.
13   So, I went to my guidance counselor. She praised me
14 for being able to juggle all my responsibilities at home and
15 still keep up my grades. She said that someday I'd get into
16 a really good college because they look for people who are
17 mature and dependable and organized and high achievers
18 ... just like me. College? How did we all of a sudden get to
19 the topic of college? What about now? What about just
20 being a kid?
21   I want to be able to sleep through my alarm and have
22 somebody wake *me* up for a change. I want to mess up on
23 a quiz and have someone hug *me* and tell *me* that I'll do
24 better next time. I want to watch TV while somebody *else*
25 puts food on the table. Don't I deserve what everybody else
26 has? Can't I please ... just once ... just be a kid?
27
28
29
30

Tree House

1   No, Daddy don't! Please don't take it down, please! If
2 you think it's that much of an eyesore, I'll paint it! Name
3 the color. I'll buy the paint out of my allowance! Only
4 please don't take apart my tree house!

5   I know you built that tree house when I was six. But, I'm
6 *not* too old for it at all! I just *use* it differently, that's all. I
7 don't know what's more important to me ... that you and I
8 built it together ... or that it's my own special place. Either
9 way you look at it, though, I can't let you touch it, Daddy.

10   Don't you remember how much fun we had putting it
11 together? Yeah, yeah — I know it drove you nuts, but that
12 made it even funnier. I'll never forget the day you came
13 home with that tree house kit. Kit? It was really a truckload
14 of lumber and a page of directions you said sounded more
15 like Martian than English! But the best part was that you
16 said that this tree house would be mine, all mine. You even
17 sent the boys into the house while we were building it.
18 Daddy, I don't think I've ever felt more important.

19   And OK, I know I'm not up there as much as I used to
20 be. There are so many things that take up my time, now:
21 school, soccer practice, flute lessons ... But Daddy, even
22 though I'm not in the tree house all the time, I know it's
23 there when I need it. Whenever I'm crying and I can't hear
24 myself think ... whenever I'm stressed and I want to be
25 alone ... whenever I'm so happy that I need a place where
26 I can laugh and sing without anybody hearing me ... I can
27 always count on my tree house. It's my special place.

28   So Daddy, please leave it up for a few more years.
29 Actually, I was kinda hoping that it'd be there forever ...
30 just in case I need it.

Angel of Peace

1   *(The actress, first asleep, wakes up with a jolt and starts*
2   *screaming. She grabs her pillow and cries into it. Soon, she*
3   *seems to calm down, to relax.)* **Thank you. I'll be all right. I've**
4   **been having such terrible dreams ever since my mom ...**
5   *(She stops crying and looks up from her pillow in surprise.)* **Who**
6   **said that? ... Wh-where are you? ... I know somebody's in**
7   **here ... Please? ... I ... I won't scream ... I promise ... You**
8   **said such kind words to me that I know you won't hurt me.**
9   **Please, come out?**
10   *(She focuses on the foot of her bed and gasps quietly in awe.)*
11   **Ah, you're beautiful! I always felt you were here ... but I**
12   **never imagined anything so beautiful! How could anything**
13   **so delicate be real? ... I'm sorry — I hope I haven't**
14   **embarrassed you ...** *(Giggle)* **Oh thank you, but I'm not nearly**
15   **as pretty as you are ... Um, do you have a name? You called**
16   *me* **by name when you calmed me from my nightmare. What**
17   **should I call** *you***? ... But I must call you something. Anything**
18   **that can soothe me like you did, anyone who could bring me**
19   **such peace deserves — Oh, how perfect! May I call you**
20   **"Peace"?** *(Giggle)* **OK, then Peace it is.**
21   **How long have you been here, Peace? ... For always?**
22   **... Even when I cried as a baby, I always felt something**
23   **ease my mind. Was that you? ...** *(Giggle)* **My Dad will never**
24   **believe this! ...** *(Listens and looks concerned.)* **Of course I**
25   **promise. I will never tell anyone if you don't want me to. I**
26   **would never, ever do anything to hurt you! Honestly! ...**
27   **Peace? Will I ever stop hurting about Mom? Will these**
28   **nightmares ever stop? ...** *(Smiling)* **Really? ... Thank you,**
29   **Peace ... Yes, I will.** *(Lies down.)* **... Good night, my Peace.**
30

Waiting Room

1   Excuse me? Have you heard anything yet? Yes, I know
2 you told me you'd let me know when you heard something,
3 but that was an hour ago. No! No, ma'am, I don't think I'd
4 like to sit down! I don't want a "nice soda pop." I want
5 some information! And would you quit calling me "young
6 lady"? I'm not that young! And if I *were*, I wouldn't be old
7 enough to be a lady!
8   Oh gosh, I'm sorry. I know you're just a volunteer.
9 You're just supposed to wait by that phone and let people
10 know when operations are over. It's a very nice job, really,
11 but it ... it's just not enough. I know it's not your fault ...
12 You're just a nice, old lady who's trying her best and —
13 There I go calling you an "old lady"! First I tell you off for
14 calling me a "young lady" and then I call you an old one!
15 Talk about foot in the mouth! I'm sorry ... I'm just such a
16 ... wreck!
17   ... No, I'm not OK. I'm very ... not OK. It's my age,
18 really. If I were a little girl, they'd leave me at home with a
19 baby-sitter who would give me lots of ice cream. I'd never
20 even *know* my sister was hit by a drunk driver! And if I
21 were older, they'd let me in there, wherever my parents
22 have been taken. I'd be closer to my sister, and I'd know
23 what the heck is happening. But here I am ... not young ...
24 not a lady ... waiting in some huge room with couches that
25 smell like medicine ... a TV stuck on the news channel ...
26 and a stranger who's trying to be very understanding ...
27 but who doesn't know anything more than I do. Omigosh!
28 It's the phone!
29
30

Allergies

1   *(The actress begins with a big sneeze. She speaks with a*
2 *stuffy nose, pronouncing each underlined m̲ as a b for comic*
3 *effect.)*
4   I a̲m a walking allergic disaster area. Oh yes, I truly
5 am̲. *(Blows nose.)* I'd be better off if I lived in one of those
6 oxygen tents, because the way I a̲m now is just ...
7 m̲iserable. And if *tonight* is a hint about m̲y future, I'll
8 probably never m̲arry ... I'll die a lonely, old lady ... in a
9 lonely glass bubble ... with m̲y little, hairless cat M̲uffin by
10 m̲y side. *(Coughs.)* Tonight was m̲y first double date.
11   M̲ichelle arrived at m̲y house early so we could get
12 ready together. I don't know what perfu̲me she brought
13 with her, but I developed this terrible rash all over m̲y
14 body! *(Scratches uncontrollably.)* I was all red and prickly
15 when the boys showed up! When I answered the door,
16 there were M̲ark and M̲atthew. They looked m̲arvelous. I
17 reached out a hand that by this ti̲me looked like raw m̲eat
18 to take the beautiful rose that M̲atthew brought m̲e. Poor
19 M̲atthew. How was he to know that roses m̲ake m̲y eyes
20 water? Within two m̲inutes flat m̲y m̲ascara was dripping
21 onto m̲y new blouse!
22   M̲atthew's dad drove us to the m̲ovies in his new
23 M̲ercury. He had one of those scented trees hanging from
24 his m̲irror. It was pine ... not good ... pine m̲akes m̲e
25 sneeze. *(Sneezes.)*
26   Since I could barely see — my eyes were all puffy
27 y'know — the others had to lead m̲e into the m̲ovie theater.
28 M̲atthew bought m̲e popcorn. They must have used a
29 preservative in the buttery-flavored oil, because I had a
30 sudden loss of balance. M̲atthew and M̲ichelle had to hold

1 <u>me</u> in <u>my</u> seat to keep <u>me</u> fro<u>m</u> slipping off.

2 When we got ho<u>me</u>, I thanked <u>M</u>atthew. From what
3 I could see through <u>my</u> swollen slits of eyes, <u>M</u>atthew
4 looked so relieved that the date was finally over, that I
5 didn't have the heart to tell hi<u>m</u> that as he walked <u>me</u> to
6 <u>my</u> doorstep, I was stung by a bu<u>m</u>blebee.

7 You really should give <u>me</u> that shot now, Doctor.
8 Fro<u>m</u> past bee sting experience, I give it only about
9 another <u>m</u>inute before I pass ... right ... out. *(Faint)*

10
11
12
13
14
15
16
17
18
19
20
21
22
23
24
25
26
27
28
29
30
31
32
33
34
35

Panic

1 Now that I'm finally home, and Kelsey is safe in her
2 bed, my heart is starting to slow down a little bit. It's been
3 pounding so hard that I'm surprised nobody saw my blouse
4 beating up and down! But I deserve it. If I had died of a
5 heart attack, even — I'd've deserved it.
6 We were at the mall, see, and Mom wanted to try on
7 dresses for some dumb wedding, and my little step-sister
8 Kelsey was getting kinda ... itchy. She was whining and
9 moaning and being a general pain in the neck. So Mom
10 suggested that I walk Kelsey down to the toy store, and
11 she'd meet us in fifteen minutes. I really hate it when she
12 pushes Kelsey on me. I mean, she became my *instant*
13 sister less than a year ago, and now I'm expected to bend
14 over backwards for her. But, anything was better than
15 watching Mom try on a bunch of old lady dresses.
16 At the toy store Kelsey started yanking my arm so hard
17 that I thought she'd pull it outta the socket. I let go for one
18 minute — two at the most — so I could look at the video
19 games in peace. I reached for Kelsey's hand and ... and it
20 wasn't there! I ran all around the store, screaming Kelsey's
21 name! I imagined all sorts of terrible things like some big
22 guy in a stocking mask carrying Kelsey away with his hand
23 over her mouth and her little eyes streaming with tears! I
24 whipped around the corner into the next aisle ... and there
25 ... hugging a baby doll ... was Kelsey.
26 "Wook!" she said happily, "It's a wittle sister just for *me!*"
27 *(Big pause)* That baby doll cost me a whole month's
28 allowance. But ... oh ... was it ever worth it.
29
30

Wallflower

1   Girls are definitely the superior sex. Well, smarter,
2 anyway. Isn't smarter superior? Yeah, I was right the first
3 time.
4   Anybody who falls for Marylou's act has to be brain
5 dead. And you know what? Every boy I've seen around her
6 starts babbling and drooling like an idiot. Ironically, that
7 makes Marylou, the con artist, pretty darn smart, doesn't
8 it? I hate her, but ya gotta admire her all the same.
9   She wears these little bitty clothes that I'd never be
10 caught dead in. But who am I to criticize? *She's* the one
11 with all these guys bowing down at her feet. Meanwhile,
12 I've got my pride, but no boyfriend. *She's* the one who
13 plays all the nauseating, flirty games and gets the phone
14 calls every night. *I'm* the one who is up front and honest,
15 but the only time a guy calls *me* is when he forgets an
16 assignment.
17   What's wrong with this picture? I'm not half bad to
18 look at ... I get good grades ... I'm even an awesome
19 dancer! Marylou, on the other hand, is no cuter than I am,
20 struggles in school, and can't dance her way out of a paper
21 bag! *I* have the reputation of being someone who's really
22 going places in life. Marylou's reputation is that she's a ...
23 well ... let's just say that her mother would *not* be happy
24 if she knew.
25   But the crazy part is ... there's Marylou having fun out
26 there on the dance floor ... and here *I* am standing off to
27 the side like a potted plant. What is *wrong* with these guys,
28 huh?
29
30

Bumper Car Emotions

1   On TV everybody always knows what to say. I sure
2 could've used a scriptwriter this afternoon. Not only was it
3 my first funeral ... not only was it a suicide ... but he was
4 the brother of my best friend, Sam. Mom didn't want me
5 to go, but I sort of felt I had to ... you know?
6   I felt like my mind was going to explode. Still do. What
7 do you say when someone dies? What do you say when it's
8 someone who's so young? He was in his first year of
9 college! What do you say when one of your classmates is
10 sobbing with grief? What do you say when he's a boy you
11 care about, but who you've never really talked to much? My
12 head was a race track and my thoughts were bumper cars.
13   The worst part ... and I've never told this to anyone else
14 before ... the thought that upsets me the most is that I don't
15 feel sorry for Sam's brother. I hate him. I know you think
16 I'm a monster, but I can't help it. I think he was mean and
17 cruel and selfish and evil. I do! I don't care how bad things
18 were going in college — he didn't have to punish the rest
19 of his family for it. My friend Sam will never be the same
20 again. Never! You should have seen him! And his parents
21 are in even worse shape! If life was that bad for Sam's
22 brother, why didn't he talk to someone? There are people
23 who can help! Teachers and priests and doctors! His own
24 pain may be over now, but it's only just beginning for his
25 family. I think he was a thoughtless, self-centered coward!
26   I just didn't know what to say. Other people were
27 saying, "I'm sorry" or "He's at peace now" or "Rest his
28 soul." I couldn't say anything because if I did, I'd have
29 said, "He makes me so mad!" So instead ... I didn't say
30 anything.

Butterscotch

1   *(The actress places a small bowl on the floor.)* **Butterscotch!**
2   **Butterscotch! Here's your favorite food — real tuna! Come**
3   **on, baby! Here, kitty-kitty-kitty!**
4   *(Forlornly)* **Oh, Butterscotch, it's been two days! Where**
5   *are* **you? Was it something I did? Something I said? I know**
6   **I've been taking you for granted lately. Maybe that's it.**
7   **Last time you rubbed against my leg, hoping for a kitty**
8   **treat, I guess I ignored you. But Butterscotch, I was trying**
9   **to study for a science test!**
10   **I miss all the annoying little things you do,**
11   **Butterscotch. You know how you plop right down on my**
12   **stomach when I'm trying to sleep? Well, now I realize that**
13   **I can't fall asleep at** *all* **without you. I need your little**
14   **toaster body to keep my toes warm at night. And I miss**
15   **walking past the bookcase where you lurk quietly ready to**
16   **bat my hair as I pass. It's not the same coming home from**
17   **school anymore, either. No furry little face pounces on my**
18   **book bag as soon as I open the door.**
19   **Come home, Butterscotch! Where could you be? There**
20   **are raccoons out there — dogs —** *cars*! **Oh, I can't stand**
21   **to even** *think* **about it! No! Nothing happened. You're just**
22   **torturing me because I don't appreciate you enough. And**
23   **you're right. Did you hear me, Butterscotch? You're right!**
24   **Things will be different from now on. I swear! Just please**
25   **... come home.**
26
27
28
29
30

The Locket

1   *(Exhausted, plops into a chair.)* **Oh.** *(Groans.)* **Everything**
2   **hurts. I've been working so hard to pay back Mr. Abbott at**
3   **the jewelry store. The toughest part is trying to raise the**
4   **money without Mom finding out.**
5   **I'm not old enough for a real job, you know, like**
6   **working at a store. So I've been weeding people's gardens,**
7   **carrying groceries, walking dogs ... anything I can get!**
8   **Mom thinks I've suddenly turned into the model student**
9   **because I spend so much time at the library. Little does she**
10 **know!**
11   **It's because I'm such a spoiled brat that I'm in this**
12 **mess in the first place. When I want something, there's no**
13 **stopping me. I have to learn that no means no.** *(Groan)* **Oh**
14 **look, these feet look like swollen balloons.** *(Massages them.)*
15   **You see, I borrowed Mom's locket. No, I took it.**
16 **"Borrow" is the spoiled brat word for "steal." It's the only**
17 **memory my mom had of my father. She threw out**
18 **everything else. It was a tiny gold heart with an even tinier**
19 **blue sapphire. Inside was some engraving, so small that**
20 **you could barely read it. It said, "Always, Alan." ... Liar.**
21   **All I wanted to do was wear it a while. I don't have**
22 **anything of my own from him and ... and every now and**
23 **then I wear it to ... to feel an eency-weency part of him next**
24 **to me. But it must have fallen off because I can't find it**
25 **anywhere! How could I tell Mom that I lost the only thing**
26 **in the world from my dad she was willing to keep?**
27   **Lucky for me, I'm good at art. I drew a picture of the**
28 **locket and gave it to Mr. Abbott at the jewelry store. He**
29 **made such a good copy that even I can't tell the difference.**
30 **At least the new locket sorta stands for hard work and**

1 **love, even if the old one didn't. Poor Mom, she deserves**
2 **it.** *(Walks painfully off.)*
3
4
5
6
7
8
9
10
11
12
13
14
15
16
17
18
19
20
21
22
23
24
25
26
27
28
29
30
31
32
33
34
35

Monologs
for Guys
(Serious)

Loyalty

1   Yeah, I hit 'er. Yeah, yeah, I know I shouldn't have hit
2 a girl. Yeah, yeah. Will you lay off me? I know all that!
3   I don't care if they keep me after school, or make me
4 clean desks, or whatever ... I'm not apologizing. Nobody
5 can make me. She called me a retard.
6   I could take it if she called me a geek ... or a nerd ... or
7 anything else. Heck, if she had hit me first, I probably
8 would've just stood there. But she called me a retard ...
9 and she knows what that means to me.
10   I know it's not a bad thing. I guess I know better than
11 anybody. My sister is ... learning impaired ... you know ...
12 slow. But she's the best little kid there is, and I'd clobber
13 anyone who says it's not true! She likes everybody. It
14 doesn't matter if you're smart or stupid or short or fat. She
15 likes a person because ... because she doesn't judge
16 anyone. I don't know anybody else like that. She's always
17 asking me if she can help, too. It doesn't matter if it's
18 taking out the garbage, or cleaning up my room, or even
19 emptying the cat litter. She just likes to be with me, that's
20 all. My sister is the most special person I ever met. I guess
21 that's why I blow up whenever anyone makes a retard joke.
22   I should have said, "Thank you. Thank you for calling
23 me a retard ... because that means I'm nice ... and kind ...
24 and that I like everybody." Yeah, that's what I *should* have
25 said ... the big jerk.
26
27
28
29
30

War Games

1   It was the weirdest thing. I was pulling on my
2 camouflage pants, just like I do every day after school ...
3 and all of a sudden, I couldn't finish changing my clothes.
4 What will I tell the other guys? They'll never understand.
5 They'll call me a wimp.
6   It's all because of that stupid news program that my
7 dad was watching last night. Usually, I'm not allowed to
8 watch TV during my homework hour, but I needed to ask
9 him a question about math. When I looked up from the
10 long division problem he was explaining, I saw all of these
11 dead bodies on the TV. I knew about the war going on, but
12 I just never thought about ... well ... the dying. You know?
13 There were so many of them — the bodies. They covered
14 a whole field. All you could see were dirty clothes with
15 arms and legs poking out ... and they were covered with
16 blood. Then the camera got real close to one little lump in
17 the middle of all of the bodies. I thought I was going to
18 vomit. It was a little kid ... a dead little kid ... right there
19 in the middle of a whole sea of bodies. How can they show
20 that on the news, anyway? It should be against the law.
21   So there I was, getting ready to play "War" with the
22 guys ... and I couldn't do it. It's not like we hurt each other.
23 It's all pretend. Everybody knows that. But I just can't get
24 the picture of that little kid out of my mind. I hate the
25 news.
26
27
28
29
30

Big Man

1   *(Laughing in response to a joke)* **Good one! Pretty funny,**
2   **man!** *(Stretching noise)* **Oh yeah ... this is living ... this is**
3   **definitely cool!**
4   I can't believe your parents agreed to let you move in
5   here! Not that it doesn't make sense, if you know what I
6   mean. Now that your brother's married and moved out, it's
7   logical that your folks wouldn't want this place to go to
8   waste. And it's not like you're far away or anything. Oh man!
9   I am so freaking jealous! A basement apartment! Do you
10   have any idea — the slightest clue — how totally cool this is?
11   You can put your feet up on the table! You can play
12   your video games as loud as you want! You can even — Oh
13   man, is that a refrigerator? You've got your own
14   refrigerator? I think I've died and gone to heaven!
15   What? ... uh ... No thanks, man ... I think I'll pass. No,
16   that's OK ... I'm not really thirsty. No, no, beer's cool ...
17   it's just that I don't want my mom to smell it on my breath
18   when she picks me up ... Chewing gum? Yeah, that's a
19   great idea ... but, hey, I have a really big science test
20   tomorrow and ... and ...
21   Hey! Who are you calling a baby? You'd better take
22   that back or I'll rearrange your face! ... Yeah? ... Listen
23   you, your parents let you move in here 'cause they think
24   you can handle living like a man. *You're* the one acting like
25   a baby, butt-head. Here you are, being handed a dream
26   come true, and the first week that you have to prove how
27   mature you are ... you want to ruin the whole thing by
28   getting caught with beer? And *you're* calling *me* a baby?
29   So long, big man. How about you give me a call when you
30   grow up? *(Storms out.)*

Praying, Sort Of

1   I ... I've never prayed before. Mom and Dad didn't
2 really push that kind of stuff. But I feel like there's nothing
3 else for me to do.
4   You see, I get this phone call from Andrew. I say, "Hey,
5 Flubber, where have you been? It's like you dropped off the
6 face of the earth or something!"
7   So he tells me he's been pretty sick, in and outta the
8 hospital. He says he's getting so bored that he wants to
9 punch the wall in. His parents said I can visit, so would I
10 like to stop over and hang out for a while? Then his mom
11 gets on the phone. She sounds all funny-like and asks if
12 she can speak to my mom. I say, "Sure," but I'm thinking,
13 "weird."
14   A couple minutes later, Mom knocks on my door. She
15 asks if I'm OK with this Andrew-thing. "Sure, why not?"
16 She tells me he's ... he's got cancer. He's gonna seem real
17 different ... and that everybody's hoping for the best. Then
18 she juts forward like she's going to kiss me or something,
19 stops in mid-air, and says she's gotta get the car keys.
20   So when she drops me off, I'm feeling, you know, like
21 ... like not knowing what to expect. His mom opens the
22 door. When she sees me, she gives me this huge hug. It
23 was kind of sad, but nice.
24   Then I hear, "Hi." Andrew was sort of yellowy-white.
25 The strangest part was his hair — it *wasn't*! Not one little
26 hair! Not even an eyebrow! I tried not to stare. But you
27 know what was cool? Andrew. The *inside* Andrew. He was
28 so happy to see me. We played cards, joked around about
29 kids we know ... nothing really "deep" or anything ... just
30 the regular stuff. It was fun!

1   But ... now that I'm back home ... I'm not feeling the
2 fun part anymore. I'm thinking about Andrew. I'm
3 scared, and I wish like heck that I could *do* something.
4 I thought about talking to Mom ... but that would just
5 worry her.
6   *(Looking upward)* **Please, please help Andrew to get**
7 **better ...**
8
9
10
11
12
13
14
15
16
17
18
19
20
21
22
23
24
25
26
27
28
29
30
31
32
33
34
35

Mechanic-to-Be

1   Look at the time! Mark will be here any minute! Oh boy,
2 how did I get myself into this mess? Don't just sit there.
3 You're partly to blame, too, ya know. Some help you are.
4   I just wanted to see how it works! Mark oughta
5 understand that, right? I mean, after all, he's the one who
6 got me interested in taking things apart. I used to beg to
7 do anything he did. I guess since he's older, I figured he
8 was some kind of a hero or something. I remember when
9 Dad got Mark his first tool set, and I had to drag out my
10 little plastic set, too. He'd dismantle his bike, and I'd
11 pretend to take apart my tricycle. He'd open up Mom's
12 toaster, and I'd fool around with the door of the bread box.
13 It was always so cool to watch how every screw, every
14 wire, every gear fit together so perfectly. Machines
15 fascinate me. Each little part depends on the next. If just
16 one little part is out of whack, it can shut down the whole,
17 entire machine!
18   When Mark got this for Christmas, I nearly busted a
19 gut! Some of it was jealousy, but mostly, I just had to
20 figure out how this thing works! I don't understand what
21 went wrong. Do you? I mean, we placed every part in a
22 logical order on the rug. We spent more time studying each
23 little nut and bolt than we ever do for any ol' test in school!
24 We replaced every little item carefully into the casing. We
25 slowly screwed the back on again ... So why the heck do
26 we have three extra parts still lying on the rug?! Oh man,
27 am I in trouble!
28
29
30

Diary

1   *(The actor is lying on his back, thinking. He bursts up,*
2   *throws his pillow to the floor and kicks it Upstage.)* **I can't**
3   **decide! I've thought over every inch of this problem and**
4   **it's a lose-lose situation. If I don't tell, I lose. If I tell, I lose.**
5   **I wish I hadn't been such a jerk and read Melissa's**
6   **diary ... No, I don't. Maybe it's good I was such an idiot**
7   **brother because if I hadn'ta read her stupid diary, I'd never**
8   **know she's doing drugs. Maybe I can help her outta this**
9   **somehow. This stinks! I was hoping I could find out some**
10 **dirt like who she was kissing, or if she knew any gossip, or**
11 **if she wrote anything about *me*. Never in a million, billion**
12 **years did I think I'd find out anything this ... intense. I**
13 **never really wanted to hurt Melissa ... I just wanted to be**
14 **a pain ... that's all. What do I do now?**
15 **One side of me says to put the diary back and pretend**
16 **that none of this ever happened. But if I do, Melissa could**
17 **hurt herself, or get caught by the police, or even die. She**
18 **may be a spoiled, bossy, know-it-all ... but she's my sister.**
19 **I gotta protect her sorry butt.**
20 **The other part of me sorta wants to tell Mom and Dad**
21 **— not because I like tattling ... well, not *this* time anyhow**
22 **... but because they'd be able to stop Melissa before things**
23 **get too dangerous. If I tell, though, she'll be in tons of**
24 **trouble, and she'll never speak to me again.**
25 *(Deep breath)* **I think I'd rather have a sister who wishes**
26 **I was dead ... than a dead sister I wish was alive.**
27
28
29
30

Too Short

1   Lunch. I hate it. Lunch period is the only time of the
2 day when we're thrown into the same room with ... with ...
3 the older kids. What's the big deal, you say? Well, look at
4 me! Sure, I'm good-lookin'. Sure, I've got a great sense of
5 humor. But take off the blinders and look! I'm way down
6 here ... and the older kids are way, *(Looks upward as though*
7 *peering at a giant)* way up there!
8   Now, don't go sounding like my mom: *(Mimics)* "Oh
9 Billy," I hate that — it's *Bill!* Anyway, she says, "Oh Billy,
10 it just takes time. You'll be towering over those boys in a
11 year or two." Doesn't she get it? Words like that aren't too
12 comforting to a guy who's always staring at people's
13 chests! Actually, it's not so bad when I'm around Marie
14 McDonald ... Nah, I won't go there. Words like that don't
15 help when the older guys stuff me into my locker, and it's
16 not even a tight fit! You don't understand what it's like to
17 have your hair ruffled like a poodle by every female teacher
18 in the building!
19   Lunch! The nightmare of every guy who ... who's
20 waiting to be a tower in a year or two. Lunch! It's enough
21 to make a guy lose his appetite.
22
23
24
25
26
27
28
29
30

Part of the Miracle

1   I'm gonna be a doctor. Don't look at me like I have
2 three heads! I've made up my mind. Oh and don't gimme
3 the line about how many years it'll take. I know all about
4 it. And I've heard the routine about how kids are always
5 changing their minds ... Blah-dee-blah-dee-blah.
6   See this scar? Skiing accident. Pretty gross, huh? The
7 bone was sticking right out. Who do you think fixed me
8 up? Santa Claus?
9   Did ya see this one over my eye? Half an inch lower and
10 Johnny Murphy's scissors would've gone right into my eye.
11 I would've had to wear one of those pirate patches for life!
12 And who sewed me together again? The tooth fairy?
13   Look down my throat. See any tonsils? Nope! Oh, and
14 check out my earlobe! Almost lost it. Neighbor's dog. Look
15 at my thumbnail. Pretty bumpy? Fish hook. Man, I'm a
16 walking disaster. And who could I always count on? Doctors!
17   But none of those things come even close to what
18 happened to my little, baby cousins. We always loved 'em.
19 I mean, heck, they were always so cute and goofy. We
20 would've loved them no matter what. But it has to be hard
21 to want to be your own person, do your own thing ... if you
22 share the same liver with your twin. You know? All I know
23 is that it's as close to a miracle as I've ever seen. They go
24 into the hospital ... just one little body ... everyone all
25 worried and crying ... and then they come home ... two,
26 separate, great little guys.
27   I've gotta get in on that magic — I do! I don't care how
28 long it takes; *I'm* gonna be part of those miracles, too!
29
30

Teacher Crush

1   I must be some kind of a sicko. Really, I'm worried. I'd
2 talk to Dad about it 'cept then *he'd* think I was a sicko, and
3 he'd send me to a doctor for sickos, and that'd just make
4 me feel ... well ... sick.
5   You know that new student teacher? Miss Marshall?
6 Well, she's lookin' kinda ... good ... to me. See? See?
7 Sicko! I'm telling you, I don't know what it is! She's gotta
8 be ... what ... twenty-three, twenty-four? What am I lookin'
9 at old ladies for? But I can't help it.
10   First of all, her clothes fit her ... much, much, much
11 better than the girls our age. She's more of a ... babe ...
12 than those girls, but less of a ... a mom-type than the
13 regular teachers. Oooohhhh, there's definitely something
14 wrong with me.
15   I'd never ... ever ... *say* anything ... *do* anything. I'm
16 not *that* mentally ill ... but I can't help ... lookin', that's all.
17 And I gotta tell you that it's really driving me nuts!
18   I end up thinking about her when I'm supposed to be
19 taking a test ... I start to see her in the hallway when she's
20 not really there ... I even stay after class to ask her for
21 extra help, which is totally crazy because I already know
22 the stuff! See?
23   It's off to the loony bin for me. I'm due for the funny
24 farm. Yup, time to join all of the other pistachios at the nut
25 house! *(Groan)*
26
27
28
29
30

The Bully

1   *(It is better if the actor does not look the part, allowing the*
2 *audience to use imagination.)*
3   Had enough, Sucker? Aw, da wittle baby have a boo-
4 boo? OK guys, you can let 'im go ... for now.
5   Well, pretty boy, I hear ya just transferred a couple-a
6 days ago. Been watching the football coach workin' with
7 ya. Yo! Nobody likes a show-off ... ya hear, man? Ya gotta
8 play by the rules if ya want to fit in here, chum. Watcha
9 supposed to do is sit back an' watch for a while ... see who
10 plays what ... and then fill in where you're needed. You
11 don't go walkin' right in and try for the star position. Ya
12 know what I mean? It ain't ... nice. An' us guys ... we see to
13 it that everybody on the team is ... very, very nice. Or else.
14   An' another thing, Lover Boy, what's with you and the
15 chicks? You waltz in here all polite and gentleman-like —
16 it's enough to make a guy puke — and the girls fall for it
17 hook, line, and sinker! What is with this "May I help you
18 pick up your books?" line? You think you're on *The Brady*
19 *Bunch*? But the skeeviest part is that the girls like it! Ugh,
20 it gives me the willies. Listen, Geek, you're making the rest
21 of us guys look bad. And we're not about to start acting all
22 macho-gushy like *you*, so you'd better start acting like one-
23 a *us*. Treat a girl like she's your little brother. Get it? It's
24 what they expect.
25   Now, you've got *one day* to change your tune and act
26 like everybody else. Twenty-four hours. Me and the guys ...
27 we'll be watching.
28
29
30

Couch Potato

1   Um ... Mr. Heller? ... Yeah, well ... I really want to thank
2   you so much for the Journalism Award ... I've learned so
3   much being your junior editor. Honestly, Sir, just seeing my
4   name on the school newspaper and ... and getting to work
5   with you so often after school ... well ... they're the only
6   awards I really need. Seriously.
7   And anyway, Mr. Heller ... I can't make it to this
8   evening's Awards' Ceremony. But I wanted to be sure that
9   I told you how ... how super grateful I am ... so, I hope you
10   understand. Well, bye, Mr. Heller ... I hope you have a
11   good summer and ... Excuse me? Oh no, Sir, I *do* want to
12   come to the Awards' Ceremony. Honest! It's my dad. He ...
13   well ... he doesn't want to take me ... that's all. My dad ...
14   he thinks it's kind of a waste of his time ... Oh yeah, I told
15   him I was getting the Journalism Award, but ... well ... he
16   said that if it's just a piece of paper, or a hunk of metal,
17   that the school could send it to me. He said he works hard
18   all day, and that when he gets home, he wants to lie down
19   on the couch, eat his dinner, and watch his TV shows. Sure
20   does love his TV shows ...
21   Oh, it's not *you*, Mr. Heller. Really. Last year Coach
22   Durham even called Dad on the telephone. Yeah, he told
23   Dad that I was pretty fast and that he'd like me on the
24   Cross Country Team. But Dad got kinda angry. He said
25   that a school team should compete during school. He
26   started yelling that he wasn't gonna waste his Saturdays
27   driving me all over the state just to run in the meets. If I
28   wanted exercise, I could walk the darn dog. Besides, he
29   couldn't miss his ball games on TV, could he?
30   *(The actor self-consciously wipes his face on his arm.)* **Nah,**

1   Mr. Heller, I'm fine ... Sure I am ... and I really do
2   appreciate the Journalism Award. Someday ... someday
3   I plan on being a newscaster. And you know why?
4   Because then, when my old man turns on his TV, you
5   know what he'll be watching? ... Me.
6
7
8
9
10
11
12
13
14
15
16
17
18
19
20
21
22
23
24
25
26
27
28
29
30
31
32
33
34
35

UFO?

1   *(Running in breathlessly)* **Dad? Dad? Oh good, you're**
2   **home! OK, OK, OK. I know I'm past my curfew, but holy**
3   **smoke, Dad, you won't believe what just happened —**
4   **nobody will!**

5   Lemme just catch my breath. I ran all the way home,
6   Dad, about two miles from the Carters' farm. It was pitch
7   dark and began thundering like it'd start raining any
8   minute. But I had to get home! I had to find you before I
9   forgot one, single detail!

10 OK, *(Deep breath)* here I go: ... all us guys thought we'd
11 play paintball in Carter's cornfield. I know I'm not
12 supposed to do paintball without telling you — I know we
13 were trespassing — I'm not denying any of that, Dad. But
14 just hear me out! OK, so the gang had just divided up into
15 teams when all of a sudden there was this incredible noise!
16 I betcha anything it's what those workers at the airport
17 would hear if they weren't wearing those earphone-type
18 things. Then, in one second flat, everything flashed a
19 whitish-orange. It got so hot I thought I'd be barbecued. In
20 fact, my skin still kinda hurts. Look, Dad! See the
21 difference between the skin that was protected by the
22 paintball goggles and the rest of my face? Sunburn — at
23 night!

24 That's when the strangest part happened. There was a
25 burst — no, a gust — of air ... so huge it blew me off my
26 feet! Next thing I knew, I was lying on my back in the
27 middle of the corn stalks. I started screaming my head off
28 for the other guys. I heard them yelling, too. I started
29 chasing around trying to follow their voices. Finally we
30 found each other. We were huggin' and saying how we

1 were so glad that we were all alive and then ... we all
2 stopped. We looked around us. Speechless. Silent. Dad,
3 we were standing in the middle of ... how can I explain
4 this ... it was a circle of pushed down, trampled corn
5 stalks, some of 'em burned and still smoking. It was a
6 circle! A giant, perfectly round circle! I swear on my life,
7 Dad! Come on! I'll show you!
8
9
10
11
12
13
14
15
16
17
18
19
20
21
22
23
24
25
26
27
28
29
30
31
32
33
34
35

Sleepwalking

1   *(Sleeping face down, arms and legs pantomiming holding*
2 *onto a tree limb, the actor begins to groan as if waking up.)*
3   **Is it morning already? Please Mom, just five more**
4 **minutes. Boy, this pillow sure feels rough. What kind of**
5 **laundry detergent have you been using?** *(Opens eyes, slowly,*
6 *looks around in confusion, then holds on for dear life.)*
7   **Yooowww!** *(Or similar exclamation)* **What — the — heck?**
8 **Where am I? ... It's a tree! ... A humongous tree!** *Mom!*
9 **Yeah right, like Mom'd be up a tree with me. OK ... be calm**
10 **... use logic ... be rational. Am I dreaming? No, I know this**
11 **is real life 'cause I've got to go to the bathroom real-real**
12 **bad. Oh man!**
13   **Hey! I know where I am! This is the big oak behind**
14 **Tommy's house! So, that's my house over there!** *(Looks up.)*
15 **Oh! Hi there, Mr. Birdie! ... Aw, take a chill pill. I'm not**
16 **planning on messin' with your stupid nest. You stay where**
17 **you are 'cause I'm sure as heck not goin' anywhere. You**
18 **know, come to think of it, it's not half bad up here! Not too**
19 **hot, not too cold. Gentle breeze. Lotsa shade. All that's**
20 **missing is a bathroom ... some breakfast ... and a ladder!**
21   **How in the world could I have climbed this high without**
22 **waking up? Sure, I've sleepwalked into Mom and Dad's**
23 **room a few times. When they woke me up, we all had a**
24 **good laugh. But a tree? That's pretty freaky, man. Hey,**
25 **there's Mom down there with Tommy's mom.** *(Waving)* **"Hi**
26 **Mom! Surprise?" Yes! — Tommy's dad's got a ladder. Just**
27 **in time, too. If I had to wait another second, I think I'd have**
28 **burst. And Birdie, it wouldn't have been a pretty sight.**
29
30

Moving

1   It's taken years to get my life just right, and just like
2 that they're goin' to flush it all away ... You're darned right
3 I'm mad. I hate them! Who? My parents! OK fine, so I don't
4 hate them as in I'll never talk to them again ... I hate them
5 as in I can't believe they're making me *move!*
6   I don't think I'm being unreasonable. I have sensible
7 gripes. I'm not the kind of guy who makes friends
8 overnight, you know. I have to ... sort of ... grow on
9 people. I have this group I hang out with here. They know
10 me. They accept me. I'm the guy who's always a beat off.
11 My folks say I march to a different drummer. But ... that's
12 OK with the guys 'cause ... 'cause we grew up together. As
13 the years passed by, we each sorta took on our own ... job
14 ... in the group. It's like we're on a TV sit-com, and we
15 each play a certain part. Am I making any sense? Take Jon,
16 for example ... he's the group jock. Sebastian? He's the
17 brains of the gang. Jason's the clown. Matt's the kindly-
18 uncle type. We go to him to ... I guess ... calm us down ...
19 you know? And me — I'm the odd one, the different one,
20 the group crazy-man. But that's OK because that's my job!
21 That's who I'm expected to be.
22   My parents just don't get it. If we move ... if I have to
23 start all over in a strange new place ... I won't be known
24 as the lovable lunatic anymore ... I'll just be seen as plain
25 weird. And ... and ... that'll be hard ... you know?
26
27
28
29
30

Chef

1   What do you mean it's "girly"? Half the great chefs of
2   the world are men! Maybe even more, I betcha. Haven't
3   you ever seen the cooking channel on cable? Well? So
4   where do you come off calling my hobby "girly"?
5   Can you even boil water, Chump? I bet if everyone in
6   the world died, and you were left all alone in the kitchen,
7   you'd starve to death! ... No, I won't take that back! You
8   take back that cooking is "girly"!
9   What about wood shop class — huh? Wait a minute
10   until I finish, Lame-brain. You called that pencil holder you
11   made "art," right? Well, when Grandma took us all out last
12   week to that fancy-schmancy restaurant, and you ordered
13   the Chicken Flambé, wasn't *that* art? The chicken was
14   flaming and crispy! And all around it were vegetables, all
15   colors of the rainbow! And the meat was so tender it
16   almost fell off the bone ... What? ... Shut up, you moron,
17   I'm not in love with a chicken! But *you* sure seemed to be,
18   considering you practically licked the plate!
19   Aw, you don't know what you're talkin' about. But
20   before you leave, Turkey, how 'bout lookin' in the
21   refrigerator. Go ahead, open it up. See? I made that cake
22   this afternoon. Too bad you think cooking is "girly." That
23   probably means you won't be wanting any ... even though
24   it's chocolate layer ... Oh really? I *thought* you'd have a
25   change of heart!
26
27
28
29
30

About Kelly

1   Mom? Gotta sec? Yeah ... well ... I wanted to talk to you
2   about Kelly. No, I'm not just ratting on my sister again.
3   Well, I *am*, but this is different. Mom, would you please just
4   put down the laundry for a minute? I'm trying to talk to you!
5   Yes, I *am* upset! Man, Mom, what does a guy have to do
6   around here to get you to *listen* to me? OK ... well good.
7   I think ... I think there's something really wrong with
8   Kelly. I tried to talk to her about it, but she says I'm butting
9   in. She said that I should quit being such a pain and get off
10 her back ... No, Mom, I'm *not* just tattling again! Geez!
11 And Mom, she said if I mentioned anything to you or Dad
12 that she'd never speak to me again. This ... this is very
13 hard for me, Mom. I've thought a lot about it, and ... and
14 it's just something I've gotta do.
15   Mom ... Kelly's throwing up all the time! No, she's not
16 sick. Well ... not like the flu or anything. That's what's so
17 weird ... She's not sick that way ... but she throws up all
18 the time ... on purpose.
19   ... Why do you immediately think I'm wrong, huh? Why
20 do you automatically figure that there I go making up
21 stories? Did you *ever* think that maybe *you're* wrong? Did
22 you? Did you ever think that maybe — just maybe — I
23 might know what I'm talking about? Mom, wake up! ... No,
24 I'm *not* being rude! Well, OK, I am a little, but what else
25 can I do to get you to open up your eyes?
26   Kelly goes into the bathroom all the time and
27 upchucks! Once she left the bathroom door open just
28 enough for me to see in. We had all just finished dinner.
29 Then, she walked into the bathroom and threw up just like
30 it was a regular part of her day, Mom ... like it was as

1 normal as brushing her teeth. And ... and no one around
2 here seems to know what the heck is going on!
3   Do you hear what I'm saying? It's so frustrating,
4 Mom, 'cause you won't take me seriously, and I'm
5 scared! Really, really scared.
6
7
8
9
10
11
12
13
14
15
16
17
18
19
20
21
22
23
24
25
26
27
28
29
30
31
32
33
34
35

Fire

1   *(The actor walks On-stage, takes his time walking around,*
2 *looking at the suggested, charred remains of a house fire. He*
3 *pantomimes kicking something.)*
4   This is it? This is all that's left? That's impossible! Dad
5 says it's a blessing that we're all alive. Mom is grateful that
6 none of us were at home. What's wrong with them? Are
7 they living on another planet? Don't they understand? This
8 was our house! Our home! And now it's ... nothing.
9   I remember hearing the sirens and fire engines while I
10 was in school. All us kids were laughing, saying things like,
11 "Why couldn't it be the school? We could use a vacation
12 about now." Dude, if I had any idea that it was *my* house,
13 I'd ... I don't know what.
14   I can't even make out the rooms anymore. Top floor
15 musta caved in, fallen down. What a mess! I wonder where
16 my room is. And my bed. You know, I first had a crib in
17 that room ... can you believe it's been that long? Then I
18 had a little metal bed with high sides that I used to pretend
19 was a tank. Pretty funny? Then I moved up to bunks ... and
20 finally a real bed. It was so cool. I could roll over twice and
21 not even reach the edge. But it's gone. Everything. All my
22 stuff! My clothes, my books, my collections — everything.
23   Oh man! *(Sits on the ground.)* It's like looking at the
24 world's worst joke ... or my whole life in an ashtray ... or
25 the end of the world.
26
27
28
29
30

Piercing

1   Aw Dad, why not? I'm a man now! ... Hey Dad, I don't
2   think it's appropriate to laugh when I'm talking seriously,
3   here. OK, that's better.
4   You've always told me that my body is a temple, right?
5   'Member all those chats about how drugs and alcohol
6   weaken the temple until it comes crashing down? And how
7   clean living and exercise strengthens my temple from the
8   inside out? Yeah, well, I listened to you, Dad. I heard
9   everything you taught me. And ... now ... I want to
10   decorate my temple!
11   It's no big deal, Dad. Everybody's doin' it! And the
12   piercing parlor is really clean! They sterilize all their tools!
13   And you should see the guys who work there, Dad. *They're*
14   *pierced all over their bodies, and they're healthy as can be.*
15   Look, I'll make a deal with you. I'll let *you* pick the
16   body part that I'll get pierced. How fair is that? There's so
17   many places to choose, Dad! Any place on the ear ... either
18   ear ... both if you like! We can go for the eyebrow! How
19   'bout the nose — you can pick the side or the center! The
20   lip? The tongue? The belly? Just one thing, Dad, I draw the
21   line when it comes to my chest. That's too weird, even for
22   me.
23   Dad ... Dad, that is not funny. Dad, I do not appreciate
24   ... Dad, I mean it ... *(Sigh)* **So much for our man to man**
25   **talk!** *(Shrugs and mopes out.)*
26
27
28
29
30

Anachronism

1   I'm nothing like the other guys my age. I'm an
2 anachronism. That's the first difference — I'm probably the
3 only kid in my class who even knows what that is! An
4 anachronism is something that is out of time or out of
5 place. I just don't seem to fit in. And the reason is patently
6 clear: they call me The Walking Brain.
7   It's not like I flaunt my intelligence ... if anything I'm
8 always holding back so that I don't say anything that the
9 other guys could satirize ... I mean, make fun of. But I feel
10 as though I'm always editing myself ... as though it's
11 mandatory that I hide the *real me*.
12   Yesterday epitomized my alienation of my peers. I ... I
13 mean that yesterday I blew it again and made everybody
14 hate my guts. Since the holidays are upon us, our teacher
15 showed us the classic film, Dickens' *A Christmas Carol*.
16 Afterwards, all of the kids were debating whether or not
17 Scrooge really met up with a variety of ghosts or if the
18 entire epic journey had just been a dream. Without
19 thinking, I blurted out that perhaps Freud would theorize
20 that Scrooge's visions were motivated by some
21 unconscious resurgence of guilt harbored since his
22 childhood ... You could hear a pin drop. I cleared my throat
23 and whispered, "Um ... I go for the dream idea."
24   My conclusion? Being the brain bites.
25
26
27
28
29
30

Adopted

1   Yeah, yeah, so I've been in a fight. Nah, don't touch it.
2 It doesn't hurt ... not much. It's just a shiner. Geez Mom,
3 it's not like I'm gonna die. *(Wipes nose.)* No, I'm OK — it
4 stopped bleeding ... Sorry I got it all over my shirt ...
5   Yeah, I know I'm not allowed to fight ... *Nothing*
6 happened ... It was no big deal ... No Mom, I don't want
7 you talking to Jared's mother. I'll look like a total wimp
8 who needs his mommy to protect him! Besides ... I threw
9 the first punch.
10   No Mom, it's not important ... Grounded? But that's so
11 unfair! OK fine, I'm grounded. I think I'll go clean up, now
12 ... Mom, I told you ... it was no big deal. It's my fault, OK?
13 ... No, you *can't* call her, Mom. Let me handle this, please?
14   ... OK, but only if you promise not to call Jared's mom.
15 *(Deep breath before confessing)* I beat the you-know-what
16 outta him. And I'd do it again! He ... he said you and Dad
17 adopted me outta *pity*. So I popped him one right in the
18 mouth. And then I don't know what came over me. I just
19 started swinging and yelling. I yelled, "You don't know
20 anything. They adopted me because they wanted me! Your
21 parents are stuck with *you* because they have no choice.
22 My parents *chose* to keep me because they love me!"
23   *(Awkward pause)* So ... that's what I said ... and ... and
24 anyway, Mom, he's in way more worse shape than I am ...
25 and ... and if you kinda need a hug about now ... it's OK
26 with me.
27
28
29
30

118

Happy Acres

1   *(Misleadingly polite)* **A pleasure to see you again, Sir ...**
2   **Yes, it *has* been a long time, hasn't it? I like what you've**
3   **done with the place. New couch, I see. Leather? Nice choice.**
4   **Perhaps I should get right to the matter, Sir. Mother**
5   **feels that it's time for me to begin visiting you on a regular**
6   **basis again. Since we last spoke, things were going quite**
7   **well ... for a while. I began the new prep school without a**
8   **hitch. Classes were interesting enough. The other boys**
9   **were relatively friendly.**
10   **Everything was tip-top, actually, until one night the**
11   **cafeteria served fruit salad for dessert. Just as I was about**
12   **to scoop in my spoon, a grape blinked at me! It was an ugly**
13   **green eye, and the dot where the grape had been**
14   **connected to the stem was its pupil. When I yelled out in**
15   **surprise, the maraschino cherries, shaped like little red**
16   **lips, started to laugh and mock me.** *(Becoming maniacal,*
17   *crazed, possessed)* **And you *know* what happens when**
18   **anyone mocks me!**
19   **I leaped onto the table like this! I began defending**
20   **myself with whatever weaponry I could find! Dinner rolls**
21   **were cannon balls. Pow! Pow!** *(Or similar sound effects)* **The**
22   **ketchup bottles turned into laser guns! Pshew! Pshew!**
23   *(Sound effects)* **I reached up to escape enemy lines by way**
24   **of the chandelier, but it couldn't hold my weight! It came**
25   **crashing down, bulbs exploding, little grape eyeballs flying**
26   **everywhere!**
27   *(Sudden switch; sits politely on the couch.)* **So you see,**
28   **Doctor, the school and Mother feel that it might benefit me**
29   **to revisit you and your fine staff at Happy Acres**
30   **Sanitarium ... for the time being, anyway.**

Surreal

1   I knew all about it. They told me everything in advance.
2 But knowing and seeing are two different things.
3   When Dad drove me to school this morning, neither of
4 us knew what to say. So, we just listened to the sound of
5 the tires on the road. He pulled up in front of the entrance
6 and gave me a funny look. For a second I thought we'd
7 hug, but when nothing happened, it began to feel
8 awkward. I just said, "It's OK, Dad. I'll see you soon," and
9 shut the car door.
10   It started feeling creepy as soon as the bus dropped me
11 off in front of my house. It wasn't real — it was beyond
12 real. You know what it reminds me of? Dali. Yeah, my art
13 teacher showed us a book of paintings by this really
14 twisted artist named Dali. He took real things, real objects,
15 and then did weird things to them. Like he'd have a clock,
16 but make it melt ... or paint a person, but leave his middle
17 out. You know, really weird stuff.
18   So, first I look in the garage ... no Dad's car. Then I go
19 into the house ... no newspaper waiting on his reading
20 chair. I walk into my parents' bedroom. I feel heavy like I'm
21 trudging through deep mud. I open his drawers ... empty.
22 The closet ... his half empty. I lie down on the bed. It's
23 Dad's side ... but it isn't. I look at the ceiling. This is still
24 my home ... but it isn't the same.
25   They had told me that Dad was moving out today. I
26 knew it. I accepted it. But ... it just doesn't feel real.
27
28
29
30

Bucky

1   Shhh. Be very quiet. See that baby deer? It's right
2 there under the tree that has two trunks in the shape of a
3 V. See? That's my Bucky.
4   He was hit by a car in front of my house. It was awful.
5 The mama deer and I saw the whole thing! She didn't know
6 whether to run away or stay by his side. I know she didn't
7 *mean* to abandon him. She's just a stupid deer, that's all.
8 His eyes were terrified, but he never made a sound. I
9 picked him up and took him to my dad. He knows a lot
10 about bones 'cause he volunteers for the rescue squad. We
11 put a splint on Bucky's little leg and kept him in our tool
12 shed. We got all sorts of books about deer from the library.
13 We even found the right recipe for a formula to put in a
14 baby bottle. I think Bucky's confused about who's his real
15 mama, the stupid deer who left him on the road, or me, the
16 funny animal in a baseball cap and sneakers!
17   Now that our apples are falling from our trees, the deer
18 have returned. I know Bucky would be better off with his
19 real family ... but it's hard, you know? Dad says that
20 sometimes the family won't even take a baby deer back if
21 it smells like humans. I don't know what I wish more ...
22 that his stupid mama will remember him ... or that she
23 rejects him and he's all mine.
24   Shhh! Look! It's a deer. Stay very quiet ...
25
26
27
28
29
30

About the Author

Deborah Karczewski spends her time as a writer, acting coach, mother, and veteran high school teacher. She graduated Brown University in 1977 with a B.A. in Theater Arts and Dramatic Literature and from Rutgers University in 1980 with a MFA in Acting. She combines her knowledge of teens and theater by writing pieces geared especially to young people.

Order Form

Meriwether Publishing Ltd.
P.O. Box 7710
Colorado Springs, CO 80933
Telephone: (719) 594-4422
Website: www.meriwetherpublishing.com

Please send me the following books:

_____ **Teens Have Feelings, Too! #BK-B238** $14.95
by Deborah Karczewski
100 monologs for young performers

_____ **Winning Monologs for Young Actors** $14.95
#BK-B127
by Peg Kehret
Honest-to-life monologs for young actors

_____ **Encore! More Winning Monologs for** $14.95
Young Actors #BK-B144
by Peg Kehret
More honest-to-life monologs for young actors

_____ **Spotlight #BK-B176** $14.95
by Stephanie S. Fairbanks
Solo scenes for student actors

_____ **The Flip Side #BK-B221** $14.95
by Heather H. Henderson
64 point-of-view monologs for teens

_____ **Tight Spots #BK-B233** $14.95
by Diana Howie
True-to-life monolog characterizations for student actors

_____ **Theatre Games for Young Performers #BK-B188** $16.95
by Maria C. Novelly
Improvisations and exercises for developing acting skills

These and other fine Meriwether Publishing books are available at your local bookstore or direct from the publisher. Prices subject to change without notice. Check our website or call for current prices.

Name: _____

Organization name: _____

Address: _____

City: _____ State: _____

Zip: _____ Phone: _____

❑ **Check enclosed**

❑ **Visa / MasterCard / Discover #** _____

Signature: _____ Date: _____

Expiration

(*required for Visa/MasterCard/Discover orders*)

Colorado residents: Please add 3% sales tax.
Shipping: Include $2.75 for the first book and 50¢ for each additional book ordered.

❑ *Please send me a copy of your complete catalog of books and plays.*

Order Form

Meriwether Publishing Ltd.
P.O. Box 7710
Colorado Springs, CO 80933
Telephone: (719) 594-4422
Website: www.meriwetherpublishing.com

Please send me the following books:

_____ **Teens Have Feelings, Too! #BK-B238** $14.95
by Deborah Karczewski
100 monologs for young performers

_____ **Winning Monologs for Young Actors** $14.95
#BK-B127
by Peg Kehret
Honest-to-life monologs for young actors

_____ **Encore! More Winning Monologs for** $14.95
Young Actors #BK-B144
by Peg Kehret
More honest-to-life monologs for young actors

_____ **Spotlight #BK-B176** $14.95
by Stephanie S. Fairbanks
Solo scenes for student actors

_____ **The Flip Side #BK-B221** $14.95
by Heather H. Henderson
64 point-of-view monologs for teens

_____ **Tight Spots #BK-B233** $14.95
by Diana Howie
True-to-life monolog characterizations for student actors

_____ **Theatre Games for Young Performers #BK-B188** $16.95
by Maria C. Novelly
Improvisations and exercises for developing acting skills

These and other fine Meriwether Publishing books are available at your local bookstore or direct from the publisher. Prices subject to change without notice. Check our website or call for current prices.

Name: _____

Organization name: _____

Address: _____

City: _____ State: _____

Zip: _____ Phone: _____

❑ **Check enclosed**
❑ **Visa / MasterCard / Discover #** _____

Signature: _____ Expiration
                                                    Date: _____
            (required for Visa/MasterCard/Discover orders)

Colorado residents: Please add 3% sales tax.
Shipping: Include $2.75 for the first book and 50¢ for each additional book ordered.

❑ *Please send me a copy of your complete catalog of books and plays.*

ML